CAREERS EDUCATION IN SCHOOLS

The history of the development of careers education in England and a critical examination of policy, practice and possibilities for its future

Second edition

David Andrews

This second edition is dedicated to

Bill Law (1935 - 2017), a friend and mentor for 36 years
and
Peter Andrews (1925 – 2013), my dad.

Typeset and designed by Mike Shaw.

ISBN 13: 978-1-5272-5272-1

Published by David Andrews
Second edition, November 2019.

David Andrews
50 Hay Street
Steeple Morden
Royston, Herts
SG8 0PE

07977 221281

davidandrews_ceg@hotmail.com

www.davidandrewsceg.co.uk

Contents

The author

David Andrews is an independent consultant, trainer and writer, specialising in careers education and guidance. After an initial eleven years teaching in secondary schools in Hertfordshire and Cambridgeshire, including five years as head of careers at St Ivo School in St Ives, he has spent the past 32 years, in different roles, supporting careers leaders through leading training courses, writing guidance materials, undertaking research and providing advice on policy and practice.

David is also a Fellow of the National Institute for Career Education and Counselling (NICEC) and an Emeritus Visiting Fellow at the International Centre for Guidance Studies (iCeGS), University of Derby. He was awarded the OBE for services to careers education in 2003 and in 2018 he received the Rodney Cox Lifetime Achievement Award from the Career Development Institute (CDI).

David is also co-author, with Tristram Hooley, of *The Careers Leader Handbook* (Trotman, 2018).

David lives in Cambridgeshire and, still, in hope that one day Tottenham Hotspur will win the Premier League.

Preface to second edition

Almost a decade has passed since I started writing the first edition of this book. I have retained the original preface, to explain why I wrote the book. The overall purpose I hoped it would serve remains the same: to ensure that policymakers and professional practitioners providing careers education for young people understand the past and are able to critically appraise the present as they develop and implement plans for the future.

The first edition chronicled the development of careers education in schools from its origins in the early 20th century through to its place in the statutory curriculum at the end of that century and the beginning of the next. At the time of its publication, however, the government was proposing to remove from schools in England the statutory duty to provide careers education in the curriculum. This second edition includes new chapters which describe what happened next, examine the position of careers education ten years further into the 21st century and propose steps to ensure that young people in schools have access to the career learning they will need.

In the year after the first edition appeared the provision of career guidance for young people in England underwent the biggest change it had experienced for almost 40 years. In 2012 the national careers guidance service delivered locally that had existed, in various forms, since 1974 was closed and the statutory responsibility for securing access to careers guidance for young people was devolved to individual schools and colleges. At the same time the duty to provide careers education the curriculum was removed. Since then there have been several initiatives, projects and developments that have offered support for careers education yet its position in the school curriculum remains precarious.

In this second edition the initial three chapters on the early history remain, with minor amendments and additions. A new chapter, on recent history, has been added to Part I. Part II comprises two new chapters. Chapter 5 examines critically the present position of careers education in England from the perspective of the end of the second decade of the 21st century and it includes a new section on careers leadership in schools, which replaces the case studies of careers leaders that featured at the end of the previous edition. The final chapter, looking forward to possible futures, has been revised from the perspective of 2019.

The personal motivation writing the book remains. Careers education in schools has been the continuous thread throughout my working life. I am now implementing a retirement plan. This book is for future careers leaders and those that support them through policy, resources and professional development.

David Andrews OBE
Steeple Morden, Cambridgeshire
November 2019

Preface to first edition

I have been thinking about writing a book on the history of careers education in schools in England for several years now but life and work have always got in the way somehow and provided excuses for procrastination. In the past 12 months, however, things have changed. After the May 2010 General Election my principal employers have had less money to spend on consultancy and training, with the result that more space has appeared in my diary that could be filled with getting started on the book. Not only has the change of government provided, indirectly, the opportunity to get on with the research and writing, it has also created an environment in which the book could have a new focus. The Education Bill published in January 2011 proposes to remove from schools in England the statutory duty to provide a programme of careers education in the curriculum. Careers education has always been about who gets to do what in the future but now its own future is up for debate. What better time to take stock of the history of the development of careers education in our schools than when we are about to decide what direction it should take in the future? I hope the historical perspective will be of interest in its own right but, as author, I have enjoyed the challenge of reflecting on the past and present to formulate proposals for ways forward in the 'post-statutory' era.

I have lived through most of this history. I was at school in the 1960s when careers education first appeared in the school curriculum, and first got interested in the subject when I took vocational guidance as a subsidiary option when studying for my PGCE in secondary school biology teaching at York University in the mid-1970s. I have remained involved ever since, as a teacher in the 1970s and 1980s, a local authority adviser in the 1980s and 1990s, and as an independent consultant and trainer since 1999. I intend to stick around for a few more years yet but it will be future generations of careers educators who will take the subject forward. My purposes in writing this book are so that practitioners, professionals and policy-makers who are interested in careers education now and in the future do not forget what happened in the past, or learn for the first time what went before. Equipped with such knowledge and understanding we might then have a greater chance of creating a better future for careers education and so, ultimately, for our young people.

David Andrews OBE
Bassingbourn, Cambridgeshire
August 2011

Acknowledgements

I have been a Fellow of the National Institute for Career Education and Counselling (NICEC) since 1992 and to this day both the Founding Director, Tony Watts, and the Founding Senior Fellow, Bill Law, remain sources of inspiration. I met the two of them when I was a student on the part-time postgraduate diploma in careers education and guidance at Hatfield Polytechnic from 1981 to 1983. Tony has since retired and Bill sadly passed away in 2017. Separately they encouraged me to write the first edition of this book and kindly reviewed early drafts of the initial chapters. A further source of support was Colleen McLaughlin, my mentor at the Faculty of Education in Cambridge, where I spent many happy years as an affiliated lecturer. Colleen helped me slip from delay into action.

I am equally indebted to other colleagues who generously found time to review the text of various chapters –Janet Donoghue, Anthony Barnes and Sue Barr – with a special thank you to Tristram Hooley, formerly Head of the International Centre for Guidance Studies (iCeGS), University of Derby and Director of Research at The Careers & Enterprise Company, for reviewing the new material for this second edition.

I had the pleasure of contributing to the work of iCeGS as a Visiting Fellow for the period 2014-19 and I am particularly grateful to Siobhan Neary, Head of the Centre, for her helpful feedback and advice on earlier drafts and her support in turning into reality our initial idea of publishing this second edition in association with iCeGS. The first edition was published by Highflyers Publishing and special thanks go to Mike Shaw for applying his technical and artistic skills to turn my words into this beautifully designed second edition. I would also like to thank Di Middleditch, my secretary, for her patience with my handwriting and skill in typing the entire manuscript. Responsibility for any errors and deficiencies in the text is, of course, mine.

The launch and distribution of this book have been supported by the International Centre for Guidance Studies, University of Derby.

Foreword

When David wrote the first edition of this book in 2011, I suspect he would not have envisaged the extensive changes that have occurred within careers education and guidance over the last decade. It has, to say the least, been tumultuous! David's book charts the history of careers education, which made its first appearance in the 1960s, becoming a statutory duty for schools in the late 1990s. He presents a circuitous journey of high points and low points for careers education, but always emphasising its importance in laying the foundations from which young people can construct their own career journeys.

This edition brings the history up to date. It presents a recap on the earlier history of careers education, combined with an exploration of policy and its influences and impacts resulting from the introduction of the Education Act 2011. The book presents an insightful examination of the introduction of the Gatsby Benchmarks and the role of Career Leaders in schools, offering a personal reflection on the benefits we have gained and the opportunities missed. David's strongest argument is that careers education should be a statutory entitlement for all young people: it is too important not to be. Although we have moved into a stronger position over recent years, the precarity of government policy within the field makes all arrangements fragile. The quest to regain statutory recognition for careers education often feels illusionary, and David calls for a more explicit acknowledgment of the need for discrete careers education within the Gatsby Benchmarks, which would help in achieving a more sustainable future for careers education.

David Andrews is one of the foremost experts on careers education in the UK. He has a wealth of experience developed over many years in the field and we at iCeGS have had the opportunity to work closely with him as a Visiting Fellow to the Centre. I was delighted when David asked me to write this foreword for the second edition of his book. In 2011, iCeGS had the privilege to host the book launch for the first edition. As such, we are thrilled to support and promote this second edition of the book which will be of interest to professionals, policy makers and researchers in the careers field.

David has spent much of his professional career championing the importance of careers education and the professionalisation of the role teachers can play in careers work. As he transitions into retirement it is ironic that much of his vision is starting to coalesce, but there continues to be work to be done to ensure the credibility and recognition that careers education fully deserves is realised.

Dr Siobhan Neary, Head of the International Centre for Guidance Studies (iCeGS), University of Derby.

Introduction

Careers education first appeared in the school curriculum in England about 60 years ago, and from 1998 until 2012 it was part of the statutory curriculum, but its position has never been totally secure. The Education Act 2011 removed the statutory duty on schools to provide careers education and, despite a range of initiatives to support career guidance for young people, including what has been termed the Gatsby revolution, the future of careers education in the school curriculum remains uncertain.

This book sets out to document the history of the development of careers education in schools in England, to take stock of its current position and to present possible options for its future. It is concerned specifically with that part of the curriculum that aims to develop pupils' knowledge, understanding, skills and attitudes to plan and manage their progression through learning and work, i.e. careers education. The development of careers guidance in England has been well documented but the only two major sources of reference to the history of careers education in schools were published in the 1990s (Harris, 1999; Law, 1996). The book is about both history and the future. Its intended audience includes senior leaders in schools, careers leaders, teachers of careers education, providers of initial training and continuing professional development, curriculum developers, researchers and policymakers.

In a summary of a meta-analysis of three major reviews of education in England, Professor Richard Pring, former Director of Educational Studies at Oxford University, stressed the importance getting acquainted with recent history of education in order to build cumulatively on worthwhile successes and avoid repeating mistakes (Pring, 2011). He was referring specifically to ministers, political advisers and civil servants but the principle applies equally to thought leaders and practitioners. At a time when careers education is still recovering from being removed from the statutory curriculum it is particularly important that we heed the lessons from the past and apply them to the contemporary context.

Part I charts the history of careers education in schools in England from its origins in the first half of the previous century to today. For convenience it is divided into four chapters covering: (1) the period up to the introduction of the National Curriculum; (2) the remainder of the 20th century; (3) the first decade of the 21st century; and, (4) the years since the repeal of the statutory requirement on schools in 2012.

Part II examines critically the present situation and then goes on to focus on the future. Chapter 5 looks at the position of careers education in the school curriculum and includes a section examining the relatively new concept in England of careers leadership in schools. Chapter 6 makes proposals securing a stronger position for careers education in the curriculum. Some readers will want to read the whole book, while others will be interested in particular sections. Each chapter has been written so that it can be read as a free-standing extract, and it is for this reason that the references are listed at the end of each chapter rather than all together at the end of the book.

References

Harris, S. (1999). *Careers Education: contesting policy and practice.* London: Paul Chapman Publishing

Law, B (1996). Careers work in schools. In Watts, A. G., Law B, Killeen, J., Kidd, J.M. and Hawthorn, R. (eds) *Rethinking Careers Education and Guidance,* 95-111. London: Routledge

Pring, R (2011). *Education for All: Evidence from the Past, Principles for the Future. Twelve Challenges.* Green Templeton College, Oxford: Richard Pring

Part I
The History

Chapter 1

Careers Education in the 20th Century: before the National Curriculum

For teachers of my generation the introduction of the National Curriculum in England represents a major watershed: between an era when the content of the curriculum in schools was designed by the teaching staff, albeit influenced significantly by examination syllabuses in the later years of secondary education, and a time when the subjects taught are determined by the national government. Prior to 1989 schools included careers education in the curriculum where they perceived it to be of value to pupils; over the past 30 years that decision has been overlaid with changing directions and guidance from the government of the day and the various non-government organisations responsible for implementing the National Curriculum. In reviewing the history of careers education in our schools in the last century, it is helpful to examine first, here, its origins and development up to the late 1980s and then to deal separately, in the next chapter, with the period following the introduction of the National Curriculum. This chapter describes a period of growth and coming of age for careers education.

The early years: the beginnings of careers work in schools

So when did it all start? When was the first careers lesson: who was the first careers teacher? In practice it has proved difficult to determine precisely when careers education first appeared in the curriculum in schools although we can deduce that this probably occurred at some point in the early 1960s, but then only in some schools and only for some pupils. It was at least another ten years before it featured on the timetable in most schools, and for all pupils within these schools at some point before they reached school leaving age. The second question is easier to answer. The first careers teacher to be appointed was almost certainly Stephen Foot, who took the job of careers master at Eastbourne College in 1920 (Hills, 1993). Mr Foot combined the role of careers master with teaching maths and other responsibilities including house master, rugby and rowing coach and bursar. In his autobiography (Foot, 1934) he attributes the initial spread of similar appointments in other schools to a series of articles he wrote in *The Daily Telegraph*. The reason why schools appointed careers teachers in the first half of the 20th century was to provide careers information and vocational guidance: teaching careers lessons did not come for another 40 years or so. Hitherto headmasters and headmistresses had taken on the role of providing pupils with careers advice but from 1920s onwards this responsibility was gradually passed over to the new appointment of careers master or careers mistress.

This was the period when youth employment services were established in England, described in detail by David Peck (2004) in his well-researched history of the careers service. From the labour exchanges administered by the Board of Trade, and the juvenile employment bureaux run by local education authorities (LEAs), the government established, in 1928, the Juvenile Employment Service under the central direction of the Ministry of Labour. At the end of the Second World War it was realised quite early on in the reconstruction process that an efficient youth employment service could make a substantial contribution to the new Britain and in 1948 the Employment and Training Act created the new Youth Employment Service as a successor to the Juvenile Employment Service. The intention was that LEAs would normally provide the service, leaving the Ministry of Labour to fill the gaps where LEAs failed to opt in. Administration of the service was in the hands of a new Central Youth Employment Executive (CYEE), which was comprised of officials from the Ministry of Labour, the Ministry of Education and the Scottish Education Department.

With the growth in vocational guidance services for young people the role of careers teacher started to emerge, to work with the youth employment officers in order to make sure that pupils had access to careers information and advice, and to provide such information and advice directly where pupils did not have access to youth employment officers. In 1927 the National Institute of Industrial Psychology called for every school to have "one person whose recognised duties should include the vocational guidance of pupils" (King-Hall & Lauwerys, 1955, p.383) and in 1931 the Association of Assistant Masters published a pamphlet entitled 'The Careers Master', possibly the first publication giving guidance on the organisation of careers work in schools. An early official mention of the role can be found in the Spens Report to the Board of Education: "our evidence also leads us to commend the growing practice in large schools of including on the staff a 'Careers Master' who, by establishing friendly relations with employers and employment bureaus, is able to help pupils in finding posts when they leave school. In smaller schools the position is naturally filled by the headmaster or mistress" (HMSO, 1938, p.204).

By the time the Youth Employment Service was launched in 1948 the role of the youth employment officer had extended beyond simply placing pupils into work, to providing vocational guidance. All young people were to be interviewed, including those in selective and private schools. It was further suggested that teachers should be required to provide reports for all school leavers to which the youth employment officer could refer. Thus was established the beginning of a partnership approach to providing pupils with careers guidance. This in turn extended the role of the careers teacher beyond making arrangements for the youth employment officer's visit to the school, and preparing pupils for the interviews, to collecting and collating reports on pupils, but the careers teacher was not yet teaching careers lessons. The general approach adopted by the Youth Employment Service was to present a talk to the leavers in their penultimate term and then follow this with individual interviews. The school talk covered: an introduction to the service; advice on how to choose a job and the dangers inherent in unprogressive or temporary occupations; information on the sorts of work locally; advice on applications. The talk could be described as a careers education session but it was delivered outside the timetabled curriculum and by a visitor, not the careers teacher.

This approach continued throughout the 1950s. The Youth Employment Service provided the talk and individual interviews, the careers teacher made the necessary arrangements. The careers teacher also provided careers information, largely in the form of literature published by the Ministry of Labour, the CYEE and the local youth employment offices. In its 1958 annual report on youth employment the Ministry of Labour and National Service noted that "in an increasing number of schools efforts were being made to give boys and girls a background of occupational information in preparation for the school leaving interview" (HMSO, 1958, p.2). Careers teachers were also providing some advice to pupils, particularly those staying on at school beyond the leaving age, but still the role was focused on providing information and advice, and mainly on educational choices. Careers education was yet to emerge on the school curriculum. Bill Law (1996) refers to this first stage in the development of careers work in schools as a 'supplementary service', provided not as part of the curriculum but independently of the curriculum. Careers education was not to appear as part of the curriculum until sometime into the 1960s.

1960s: careers education emerges in the curriculum

The 1960s is characterised as a time of economic prosperity, increased participation in education beyond the statutory school leaving age (at the time 15) and significant expansion in higher education. With these increased opportunities in employment and education for young people came a growth in vocational guidance in schools. The Youth Employment Service continued to offer advice to pupils from the age of 14 and more and more schools extended their pastoral care services until by the end of the decade most were advising pupils on educational, vocational and personal matters throughout the secondary stage. The focus of the work of the Youth Employment Service was still a single interview in the pupils' final year but in addition it provided help to schools with developing their careers programmes (which, at this point, comprised mainly information talks) and it disseminated occupational literature. At the same time the schools' provision expanded to include more systematic guidance to pupils on their educational choices (usually with only limited attention to the vocational implications). This shared responsibility between the external guidance service and the school's pastoral care was noted in a CYEE memorandum: "in the preparatory stages of providing pupils with careers information, and at all times when educational rather than vocational decisions are to the fore, the school should bear the main responsibility" (HMSO, 1962, p.2). The document also recognised the vocational importance of subject choices made at age 13, and that vocational guidance is not a single operation but a continuous process.

To support the development of guidance in schools the availability of training for teachers increased. In 1961 Manchester University launched a new Diploma in Educational Guidance. Further courses in pastoral care were developed at Keele, Exeter, Reading and Edge Hill. In 1959 the Ministry of Education had included in its national programme of short courses one for headteachers and careers teachers on 'Careers Guidance and the Schools'. This course proved popular and continued throughout the 1960s, led by Harold Marks, a staff inspector with Her Majesty's Inspectorate (HMI) who played a major role in promoting careers work in schools at this time.

The development of careers work in schools was given a particular impetus in 1963 by the publication of the Newsom Report *Half Our Future* (HMSO, 1963). John (later Sir John) Newsom was asked to prepare a report "to consider the education between the ages of 13 and 16 of pupils of average or less than average ability" (p.xv). Newsom advocated a more outward looking curriculum that provided an initiation into the adult world of work and recommended that each school should have a member of staff "whose special business it is to be knowledgeable about employment and further education, to organise reference and display material, and to make the essential liaison between school, parents, youth employment service and employment" (ibid., p.78).

Around this time it was felt that there was a need for an agency to maintain and disseminate careers information, particularly about the availability and educational requirements of specific training in industry and for university and college courses. The CYEE had been administering the dissemination of occupational literature but had not been able to maintain a comprehensive service. Consequently in 1964 the Careers Research and Advisory Centre (CRAC) was established by Adrian Bridgewater, who was to go on to head Hobsons Press, and Tony Watts, who was later to establish the National Institute for Careers Education and Counselling (NICEC). In its early days CRAC's mission was to advise pupils, teachers and youth employment officers, and to publish careers information. One of its first projects was to conduct a survey which found that only just over half of the schools in England had a careers teacher (Rodknight, 1969).

From this mid-point of the 1960s careers work in schools continued to expand. The Department of Education and Science (DES), which had replaced the former Ministry of Education in 1964, published a handbook entitled *'Careers Guidance in Schools'* and greatly increased the number of short courses for headteachers and careers teachers. Several universities and colleges began to offer diploma courses for teachers in guidance and counselling and some offered options in vocational guidance. Edge Hill College, for example, offered a 'careers' option on its one-year diploma and a one-term in-service training course on educational and vocational guidance for qualified teachers.

By the mid-1960s the work of the careers teacher in schools still consisted mainly of providing careers information and educational guidance, but careers lessons started to appear in the curriculum. This was partly due to a realisation that it was more efficient to pass on some careers information to class-size groups rather than have to repeat it in each individual interview, but also as a consequence of new ideas about how young people could be supported in making career decisions. The work of American researchers such as Ginzberg (1951) and Super (1957) was beginning to influence approaches to vocational guidance in Britain. They viewed occupational choice as a developmental process over time, with the individual passing through stages of vocational development – from fantasy, through interest and capacity, to exploration and establishment. Throughout this process the individual gains an understanding of themselves, an understanding of different occupational settings and tries out their self-concept in these different contexts as they make a choice. The role of guidance is to facilitate this process. Occupational choice was seen no longer as a talent-matching event, but a process of continued testing out. Peter Daws, of the Vocational Guidance Unit at Leeds University, played a major role in contextualising these ideas for career development in Britain (Daws, 1968). He saw implications not only for guidance practice but also for classroom courses for pupils, comprising activities that helped individuals to develop self-knowledge. With such thinking careers lessons were no longer restricted to talks about the options at key points of transition and practice at completing job application forms, and the term 'careers education' began to be used to describe this component of careers work in schools.

As careers education started to establish a foothold in schools, alongside careers information, guidance and early work experience schemes, so the infrastructure to support careers teachers developed. Mention has already been made of the growing number of courses at universities and colleges. Each geographical division of the DES now had its own training team, led by an HMI, leading short courses for headteachers and careers teachers. The Inner London Education Authority became the first LEA to appoint an inspector for careers education and guidance, a post which Catherine Avent, a former youth employment officer, held from 1968 to 1985. Local careers associations, where careers teachers from the schools in the area could meet to share ideas and be updated on developments, had started to emerge across the country and in 1969 the National Association for Careers Teachers (NACT) was established by its Founder Secretary Ray Heppell, a careers teacher from the North East, and under the chairmanship of Harry Dowson, a headteacher from Sheffield and major figure in the National Union of Teachers.

By the end of the 1960s careers education had arrived but had yet to become firmly established in all schools.

1970s: careers education finds a framework
DES Survey 18

In 1970 the NACT published the results of a survey of careers work in schools undertaken by Vince McIntyre (1970), a careers teacher from Middlesbrough. The findings were based on completed questionnaires from over 800 schools. Although the majority of schools had a careers teacher, careers education featured as a subject on the timetable in only one in four schools. The survey focused mainly on the facilities and resources provided for careers work and the report provided much of the

17

evidence that the NACT and Institute of Careers Officers (ICO) took with them when they met jointly with the then Secretary of State for Education and Science, Margaret Thatcher, the following year. The deputation called for the need to improve the status of careers teachers and spent quite a long time discussing the training of careers teachers. The outcome of the meeting was that Mrs Thatcher announced that there would be a sample survey of the state of careers education and guidance in schools, led by HMI in 1971-72. This resulted in the publication in 1973 of DES Survey 18 *Careers Education in Secondary Schools* (DES, 1973). The survey defined careers education as "that element in the programme of a secondary school explicitly concerned with preparation for adult life" (p.1). It went on to say that "between the ages of 13 and 17, young people pass through a zone of critical decisions, a period when they must learn to know themselves, to come to terms with their strengths and weaknesses, to make choices, reach decisions and accept the implications of those decisions" (ibid., p.1). Here we see the beginnings of a definition of careers education that still applies in broad principle today. This was to be developed later in the decade through the early work of NICEC, which will be outlined further on in this chapter.

When defining careers education in the opening paragraphs of the survey, HMI pointed to one of the major debates about the nature of careers education that had emerged at the end of the 1960s. The influence of 'self concept' theories of occupational choice on careers education programmes has been described in the previous section. These ideas, based in developmental psychology, place emphasis on individual choice. Sociologists researching school-to-work transitions at the time (e.g. Roberts, 1968) challenged this thinking and asserted that opportunity structure is the principal determinant of what jobs people enter. An academic debate ensued (see especially Roberts, 1977; Daws, 1977). The definition in Survey 18 acknowledges both perspectives by saying that the age of 13 to 17 "is a period of choice and of decision, but also of adaptation to conditions in an adult world in which occupational opportunity for young people varies considerably from area to area" (p.1). That is to say, careers education programmes in schools should help young people to know themselves and make choices, but in the context of understanding what is available to them.

The survey results were based on an extensive sample. Questionnaires were sent to over 1,000 schools with a 94% response rate, and visits were made by HMI to over 100 schools. The schools' policy and practice in careers education was assessed against three objectives:

- to help pupils achieve an understanding of themselves and to be realistic about their strengths and weaknesses;
- to extend the range of pupils' thinking about opportunities in work and in life generally;
- to prepare pupils to make considered choices.

HMI suggested that this process of achieving self-awareness, broadening horizons and preparation for making decisions should be implemented in two stages. The first stage was one of exploration, a divergent process; the second was a convergent process leading to a decision either to continue in full-time education in school or elsewhere, or to enter employment. Almost half a century later the routes and ages of transition may have changed but the processes that careers education aims to facilitate remain broadly the same.

Similarly the debate about approaches to careers education in the curriculum resonates across the last five decades. HMI referred to introducing aspects of careers education into the syllabuses for various subjects in what they call the 'infusion' model', or to giving careers education its own time in the timetable. This is a discussion point that is particularly relevant today, in the context of the Gatsby Benchmarks of good practice, where one of the eight benchmarks focuses exclusively on linking subject teaching to careers but this is not complemented by any explicit reference to making time available in the curriculum for discrete careers education. In the 1973 survey HMI found that in nearly a third of all schools there were no periods devoted specifically to careers education and in another third time was found in the leavers' courses only. Careers education was included in the third, fourth and fifth years only (equivalent to Years 9, 10 and 11 today). The survey found that 25% of schools included it for all or some pupils in the third year, 72% in the fourth year (the statutory school leaving age at the time of the survey was 15) and 48% in the fifth year.

The vast majority (94%) of schools designated at least one member of staff as 'careers teacher'. In connection with the survey HMI held a seminar for headteachers to consider the role of careers teacher.

Among the essential duties they listed:

- to act as a co-ordinator, linking the curricular and pastoral care aspects of the school
- to be fully involved in the development of the school curriculum

- to liaise with the careers officer[1]
- to establish links with higher and further education, and with industry
- to administer work experience
- to supervise the careers room and careers literature
- to plan the use of timetabled time designated for careers work.

I will return to this list in chapter 5, in a section on careers leadership in schools. The last item is one of the earliest references to careers teachers taking on the task of planning programmes of careers education in the curriculum. The headteachers stressed the importance of the careers teacher having time to plan and to train other members of staff, and of the need for clerical assistance to cope with the more routine and repetitive tasks. Many careers leaders today would suggest that these ideals have still to be implemented in practice 50 years later.

The headteachers at the seminar expressed the view that a careers teacher should have had specialist training. The survey found that in about three-quarters of schools the careers teacher had attended a short course of one to five days. In 24% the careers teacher had attended a course lasting between a week and a term and in only 11% the careers teacher had attended a course lasting one term or longer. Several universities and colleges of education at the time were offering one-year full time courses in counselling but only one was offering a diploma in counselling and careers work. Individual LEAs had taken the initiative to set up courses and in the North of England a consortium of LEAs had come together to plan the training for careers teachers. The DES continued its programme of short courses and other agencies also provided training, e.g. ICO, CRAC and NACT.

The survey provided what Mrs Thatcher asked for – a detailed picture of the state of careers education in schools. It concluded that the next decade would see a growth in careers education and the findings were referred to frequently as careers teachers and the professional associations sought to improve policy and practice in schools throughout the following ten years.

The publication of DES Survey 18 was a major event in the

[1] Towards the end of the 1960s members of the youth employment service had started to adopt the title 'careers officer' instead of youth employment officer

development of careers education in the early 1970s but it is worth recording two other events in this period which were to have implications later on. Firstly, in 1973, the NACT changed its name to the National Association of Careers and Guidance Teachers (NACGT). This was in recognition of the increasing involvement of year tutors in comprehensive schools in guidance work and part of a plan to broaden the appeal of the association. Secondly, the Employment and Training Act 1973 replaced the Youth Employment Service with the new Careers Service. From 1974 all LEAs were required to have a careers service providing careers guidance to young people. As the careers service was part of the LEA this brought about the potential opportunity for the service to become more involved in the development of careers work in schools, although the services reported to central government not via the DES but to the Department for Employment. Careers services bridge the worlds of education and employment, and where responsibility for their administration is placed within government departments can influence how their work is perceived by schools and business. This is an issue that is discussed in Peck's history of careers services in the UK (op. cit.).

Curriculum development

Once careers education had emerged in schools it started to attract the interest and attention of curriculum developers and writers of classroom materials. In the early 1970s several books, articles and resources for careers teachers were published. John Hayes and Barrie Hopson, both of the University of Leeds and later to establish Lifeskills Associates, produced a book of ideas for careers work in schools (Hayes and Hopson, 1972); Tony Watts, then Head of the Research and Development Unit at CRAC, wrote one of the first articles setting out a suggested list of objectives for a careers education programme (Watts, 1973); and Catherine Avent of the ILEA wrote a practical handbook for headteachers and careers teachers (Avent, 1974). CRAC worked with several authors to develop a series of teaching materials for careers education (Smith, 2010), including the Bull's Eye titles written by Tony Crowley, then a careers officer with Hertfordshire and who later went on to lead the postgraduate diploma in careers education and guidance course at Hatfield Polytechnic, and *Decide for Yourself*, by Bill Law, then of Reading University.

Perhaps the biggest development, in terms of the size of the writing team and the length of the project, was the Schools Council Careers Education and Guidance Project, which ran from 1971 to 1977. The aim of the project was to produce a set of careers education classroom materials for pupils aged 13 to 18.

By the time the project began the developmental approach to careers education had gained a fair degree of support.

Occupational choice was no longer seen as a single event, but as a process over time, where individuals needed access not only to information and advice but also to a programme of activities to help them understand themselves and explore different occupational roles. This approach was the dominant initial conceptual basis for the work of the project but it was not universally accepted (Bates, 1990). Within the writing team an alternative, more radical view of careers education emerged, the proponents of which wanted pupils not just to understand opportunities structures but to assess critically society and the occupational roles available and to be stimulated to act as agents of social change, particularly in the world of work. The Schools Council became concerned about the development of this more radical approach and feared that it could put it at risk as an organisation. After protracted negotiations the materials were modified significantly before publication.

The success of the project was the publication of an abundant supply of lesson activities. The Schools Council funded a substantial dissemination programme from 1978 to 1981, run by the National Institute for Careers Education and Counselling (NICEC) and directed initially by John Miller and but for most of its life by Beryl Fawcett, who was later to be appointed as an HMI for careers education. Not only did the project provide classroom materials, it also led to a shift in emphasis in careers education away from simply giving information and advice to providing a programme of activities to prepare pupils for life. However, although this approach was embraced with enthusiasm by many careers teachers their pupils were less taken with the ideas. The project's evaluation showed that most pupils would have preferred a more narrow definition of careers education, centred around local labour market information rather than more the lofty goals of career choice and self-awareness. This led in turn to teachers modifying their practices and to programmes of careers education that represented a compromise between providing information about jobs available locally and preparing pupils for working life.

Thus, in the early days of curriculum development we already see the emergence of at least three different definitions of careers education, all focused ultimately on occupational choice but differing in terms of their socio-political perspective: providing information on local opportunities (assisting pupils with initial job choices from what is available); preparing pupils for work (equipping pupils for lifelong career development); challenging existing structures (empowering pupils to influence the opportunities available). Throughout its brief history careers education has remained a contested concept (Harris, 1999): the question for practice is whether the different perspectives can be accommodated within a single programme that often sits at the margins of the curriculum.

The DOTS framework

In the middle of the decade there was an attempt to develop a model for careers education around which a consensus could be established and which has subsequently had an enduring impact (Law and Watts, 1977). In 1975 CRAC established, in partnership with Hatfield Polytechnic, a research and development organisation NICEC, with Tony Watts as Director and Bill Law as founding Senior Fellow. One of their first pieces of work was a project to examine the careers education provision in a sample of case study schools, with the aim of identifying issues for people interested in developing careers programmes to consider. It was this piece of work that led to what has since become known as the DOTS framework for careers education. They asserted that careers education aims to facilitate the development of four objectives for pupils:

- **O**pportunity awareness – an understanding of the range of opportunities within education and the world of work
- **S**elf awareness – an understanding of their strengths, needs, interests, aspirations and values
- **D**ecision learning – an understanding how to make decisions, relating opportunities to self
- **T**ransition learning – knowledge and skills to cope with transitions into the next stage of education or work.

Over the years these four objectives have been refined – for example, job seeking and application skills have been added under the heading of transition learning – and the language has changed, as we will see in later chapters, but they still today describe the basic aims of careers education.

Most careers practitioners know Law and Watts' work for the DOTS framework because of its lasting impact on curriculum guidelines for careers education over the past forty years or more, but their book also introduces another framework, this time for describing the sequence of stages for the development of careers work in schools. The authors outline four stages, each of which can be divided into two sub-stages, through which schools can pass.

Figure 1. Stages in the development of careers work in schools (from Law and Watts, 1977)

---

1. **Information**
   i 'Cardboard box'
   A collection of careers literature randomly arranged.
   ii Clerical
   A collection of careers literature forming the core of a careers resources centre with material classified and arranged to maximise the students' chances of finding it.

2. **Interview**
   i Advice
   Opportunities for students to talk to a careers teacher or careers officer about their future, where the interview is concerned with narrowing down the field and recommending particular courses of action.
   ii Counselling
   Opportunities for interviews that help individual students to analyse their own situation and to come to a decision which is theirs.

3. **Curricular**
   i Occupational education
   Timetable time is made available to present occupational information through talks, visits, films, etc.
   ii Careers education
   Opportunities planned in curriculum time to develop self awareness, opportunity awareness, decision making skills and transition skills.

4. **Integrated**
   i School guidance
   Linking the careers programme to other curricular and extra-curricular activities.
   ii Community guidance
   Linking the careers programme to resources in the community e.g. through work experience.

Looking at this framework afresh, four decades on, it is interesting to note similarities with the framework of Gatsby Benchmarks that schools are expected to follow today (Gatsby Charitable Foundation, 2014). The information stage links to Benchmarks 2 and 7 (learning from career and labour market information and encounters with education and training providers); the interview stage links with Benchmarks 8 and 3 (personal guidance and addressing the needs of each student); the curriculum stage relates to Benchmark 4 (linking curriculum learning with careers); and the integrated stage has parallels with Benchmarks 5 and 6 (encounters with employers and experiences of workplaces). What is missing is the notion of a 'stable and embedded' programme of careers education and guidance that is emphasised in the overarching Benchmark 1. That was yet to come.

I will return to the Gatsby Benchmarks in chapter 4. At the time of the Law and Watts project, only three of the six case study schools had progressed beyond stage 3i. The DOTS framework provided a basis for planning and reviewing programmes of careers education in the curriculum but such programmes were not available in all schools. By the end of the 1970s careers work in many schools still consisted only of careers information and careers guidance. Where there was a provision of careers education it was often limited to talks and 16mm films giving information about different jobs and courses.

In the latter half of the 1970s, concerns about the state of education, particularly in secondary schools, led to a debate that was to secure a stronger position for careers education in the years ahead. In October 1976 Prime Minister James Callaghan launched a 'Great Debate' about education with a speech at Ruskin College. He argued that the aims of education should be not only to equip children for a place in society but also to fit them to do a job of work. The sub-text was the need to take more control over the curriculum and to prepare pupils better for work in an increasingly technological age. Education should be responsive to the needs of the economy. In the subsequent government discussion paper careers education was named as one of five fixed points in the curriculum. This idea was later dropped but schools were still to be encouraged to provide careers education and this became a recurrent theme in the 1980s.

1980s: securing a place in the curriculum
TVEI and the curriculum debate

The Great Debate continued into the new decade, by which point the Labour government had been replaced by a new Conservative administration, headed by the former Education Minister and now Prime Minister, Margaret Thatcher. It could be argued that the debate culminated ultimately in the introduction at the end of the 1980s of the National Curriculum but before then there was to be a major government-led programme of curriculum development which strengthened significantly the position of careers education in schools.

The Technical and Vocational Education Initiative (TVEI), launched in 1983, was led and managed not by the DES but by the Employment Department. It was an attempt initially to strengthen vocational education in the 14-18 curriculum. LEAs decided whether or not to join the programme and then submitted their proposals in response to the requirements set out by the government. Once the plans had been approved the LEA received quite generous levels of funding to implement the development spread over a five-year period. Schools participated in the programme as members of a local consortium which comprised several schools in the area and the local colleges.

In the pilot phase, which ran from 1983, the programme was seen principally as a means of introducing a more technical and vocational curriculum for a particular cohort of pupils in the 14-18 age range but, by the time the initiative had moved into the extension phase, from 1987, the focus had changed to one of making the curriculum for all pupils more relevant to their future working lives. Many new vocational courses were developed, particularly at GCSE level, but emphasis was also placed on developing the core curriculum to include careers education and guidance, economic awareness, work experience and recording achievement and action planning. To return to Bill Law's three stages in the development of careers education in schools during the 1960s and 1970s we had moved on from it being seen as a supplementary service to a time when it was an optional part of the curriculum. Under TVEI we were beginning to enter the third phase, where careers education was becoming an emergent requirement, not yet by legislation but through the use of targeted funding. In return for the TVEI money schools were required to develop, among other elements of the curriculum, programmes of careers education and guidance.

Local consortia set up curriculum support groups where teachers could work together on developments and careers officers from the careers service joined these groups. LEAs expanded their support for careers education, recruiting experienced heads of careers and others to positions as development officers, advisory teachers, advisers and inspectors. Programmes of in-service training were set up, funded through TRIST (TVEI-related in-service training) budgets from the Employment Department. There was also an increase in longer courses for careers teachers across the country. In his handbook for careers education and guidance Bill Rogers (1984) lists a one-year part-time certificate course at Edge Hill College of Higher Education, a two-year part-time diploma course at Hatfield Polytechnic and one term full-time courses at King Alfred's College in Winchester, Worcester College of Higher Education and the College of Ripon and York St. John. It was a time when education policy and resources facilitated substantial growth in careers education in schools.

Throughout this period debate about the curriculum continued. In 1984 the Secretary of State for Education and Science, Sir Keith Joseph, announced that he intended to seek broad agreement on the objectives of the 5 to 16 curriculum, and in 1985 the DES published the second in the HMI series 'Curriculum Matters'. *The curriculum from 5 to 16* (DES, 1985) suggested that the curriculum in all schools should involve pupils in each of nine 'areas of learning and experience'. It also said that there were some essential issues which were not necessarily contained within subjects, but which needed to be included in the curriculum: careers education came in this category. HMI proposed that careers education should be timetabled in the later years of secondary education. They defined careers education as learning about oneself and about opportunities post-16, and using this awareness to make informed decisions – a definition based on the DOTS framework from 1977.

1987: working together for a better future

1987 proved to be an eventful year for careers education. In February the NACGT published a survey of careers work (Cleaton, 1987). 14 years previously, in DES Survey 18, HMI concluded that "the concept of careers education is not at present generally accepted or put into practice except by a minority of schools" (p.61). It had been anticipated that the DES would have followed up the report with similar surveys in the late 1970s or early 1980s, but this had not happened. In 1986 David Cleaton, Head of East Sussex Careers Service and a past President of NACGT (1981-83), volunteered to survey the current state of careers work in schools on behalf of the Association. 'Dai' Cleaton was a significant figure in careers education and guidance throughout the 1970s and 1980s, and into the 1990s. Originally a maths teacher, he took on the role of careers teacher in a school and eventually was appointed to the combined role of county adviser for careers education and head of careers service in East Sussex. In his early days he had published some of the first classroom materials for careers education and he remained passionate about improving careers education and guidance in schools.

The main findings of the survey were that, in 1986:

- 95% of schools had a careers teacher, and in 83% he or she was regarded as head of department
- 41% of careers teachers had received less than five days of training for careers work and only 7% had completed a course of a term or longer
- the vast majority of schools (about 85%) provided careers education in the curriculum for all pupils in the fourth and fifth years [now Years 10 and 11] and a further 8% provided it for some pupils in those two years, leaving about 7% of schools not providing any careers education to pupils in the final two years of compulsory schooling[2]
- a majority of schools (about 70%) provided careers education in the curriculum for all pupils in the third year [Year 9] and a further 12% provided it for some pupils
- only 16% of schools provided careers education to pupils in the first and second years [Years 7 and 8]
- the amount of time allocated to careers education in the curriculum was less than half an hour a week for the majority of pupils
- there was a trend towards careers education being organised as part of a wider personal and social education (PSE) programme
- 6 out of 10 LEAs had an adviser or inspector for careers education.

The headlines from the survey were that, although careers education had become established in the later years in most schools, there were concerns about the amount of curriculum time allocated to it and about the training of careers teachers. The sub-heading for the NACGT's report was "no training, not enough time, not enough money…..". Before going on to outline later events in 1987 it is worth noting the point above about delivering careers education as part of PSE. Curriculum models for careers

---

2 The statutory school leaving age had been raised to 16 in 1972.

education will be examined in detail in the next chapter but during the 1980s the way in which careers education was organised in the secondary curriculum changed. At the beginning of the decade careers lessons were included in the timetable either as a discrete part of the weekly timetable or as a block of lessons within a general studies programme. As schools sought to develop their curricula and to include elements beyond the traditional subject areas which focused on pupils' social and personal development, they established programmes of PSE and active tutorial work (ATW). Many schools took the decision to include careers education within such programmes, sometimes for pragmatic reasons concerned with efficient use of time, sometimes for philosophical reasons viewing careers education as part of a wider programme of lifeskills to prepare pupils for adult life.

The next event in 1987 was the publication in April of what is now viewed as one of the high points in the development of careers education in schools: a joint statement by the DES, the Employment Department and the Welsh Office on the importance of careers education and guidance *Working Together For A Better Future* (DES, ED and Welsh Office, 1987). The short booklet talked about the central role of careers education and guidance in preparing young people for adult life and the need for all parties to work together to improve the support for young people to allow them to make sound choices as they go through school and beyond. The emphasis was on partnership working, the principal partners being the schools and the careers service but supported by the LEA and working with colleges, universities, training providers, employers and parents. In the sections outlining the responsibilities of schools, the role of the careers teacher, or careers co-ordinator[3], in mobilising the school's resources was highlighted but the booklet pointed out also that all teachers, particularly those in pastoral roles, had a part to play. Referring specifically to careers education, the booklet stated that each school should provide a programme of careers education as part of the curriculum for each pupil. It went on to stress the importance of careers teachers having had up to date training, and the role of careers officers in helping to plan careers education in each school by bringing their knowledge of opportunities and the experiences of recent school leavers to complement the teachers' knowledge of the pupils and

---

3 In recognition of the fact that by the 1980s other members of staff were often teaching some of the careers lessons in their roles as PSE teacher or tutor, and providing initial information and advice, many schools began to use the job title careers co-ordinator rather than careers teacher.

pedagogy. The letter accompanying the booklet asked LEAs to review their policies for careers education and guidance and to work with schools and the careers service to improve the provision. Many LEAs responded positively to this invitation, taking advantage of the resources available through TVEI to achieve their aims. At last it seemed that careers education had come of age.

However, we were only in the spring of 1987. Throughout the 1980s the Great Debate continued and in July 1987 the Secretary of State for Education and Science, Kenneth Baker, published the government's proposals for a national curriculum (DES and Welsh Office, 1987). The consultation document, which included a list of curriculum subjects, did not include a single mention of careers education. This was despite the same Secretary of State having been a signatory to *Working Together For A Better Future* only three months previously. The story of what happened to the position of careers education in the curriculum in the remaining years of the 20th century is told in the next chapter.

References

Avent, C. (1974). *Practical Approaches to Careers Education.* Cambridge: CRAC/Hobsons

Bates, I. (1990). The politics of careers education and guidance: a case study for scrutiny. *British Journal of Guidance and Counselling*, 18 (1), 66-83.

Cleaton, D. (1987). *Survey of Careers Work: The Report.* London: NACGT/Newpoint Publishing

Central Youth Employment Executive (1962). Memorandum 28. London: HMSO

Daws, P.P. (1968). *A Good Start in Life.* Cambridge: Hobsons Press

Daws, P.P. (1977). Are careers education programmes in secondary schools a waste of time? – a reply to Roberts. *British Journal of Guidance and Counselling,* 5(1), 10-18.

Department of Education and Science (1973). *Survey 18 Careers Education in Secondary Schools.* London: HMSO

Department of Education and Science, Department of Employment and Welsh Office (1987). *Working Together For A Better Future.* London: Central Information Office

Department of Education and Science and Welsh Office (1987). *The National Curriculum: a consultation document.* London: DES

Foot, S. (1934). *Three Lives: an autobiography.* London: Heinemann

Gatsby Charitable Foundation (2014). *Good career guidance.* London: The Gatsby Charitable Foundation

Ginzberg, E. (1951). *Occupational Choice.* New York: Columbia University Press

Harris, S. (1999). *Careers Education: contesting policy and practice.* London: Paul Chapman Publishing

Hayes, J. and Hopson, B. (1972). *Careers Guidance. The role of the school in vocational development.* London: Heinemann

Her Majesty's Inspectorate/Department of Education and Science (1985). *The curriculum 5 to 16*. London: HMSO

Her Majesty's Stationery Office (1938.) *Report on Secondary Education with Special Reference to Grammar Schools and Technical High Schools*. London: HMSO

Her Majesty's Stationery Office (1958). *Report on Youth Employment during the Year 1958*. London: HMSO

Her Majesty's Stationery Office (1963). *Half Our Future*. London: HMSO

Hills, J. (1993). 'Careers guidance in independent schools'. *Education and Training*, Volume 23, Issue 10.

King-Hall, R. and Lauwerys, J.A. (1955). *The Year Book of Education, 1955: Guidance and Counseling*. London: Evans Brothers

Law, B. (1996). Careers work in schools. In Watts, A.G., Law, B., Killeen, J., Kidd, J.M. and Hawthorn, R. (eds.) *Rethinking Careers Education and Guidance, 95-111*. London: Routledge

Law, B. and Watts A.G. (1977). *Schools, Careers and Community*. London: Church Information Office

McIntyre, V. (1970). *The McIntyre Report on Time and Facilities for Careers Work in Secondary Schools*. London: Cornmarket Press

Peck, D. (2004). *Careers Services: history, policy and practice in the United Kingdom*. London: RoutledgeFalmer

Roberts, K. (1968). 'The entry into employment: an approach towards a general theory'. *Sociological Review* 16, 165-184.

Roberts, K. (1977). The social conditions, consequences and limitations of careers guidance. *British Journal of Guidance and Counselling*, 5(1), 1-9.

Rodknight, E. (1969). A survey of careers work in schools. *Journal of the Careers Research and Advisory Centre*, 4(2), 3-10.

Rogers, B. (1984). *Careers Education and Guidance*. Cambridge: Hobsons Publishing

Smith, D. (2010). *Some Sort of Bridge*. Cambridge Granta Editions

Super, D. (1957). *The Psychology of Careers*. New York: Harper & Row

Watts, A.G. (1973). A Structure for Careers Education. In Ray Jackson (ed.) *Careers Guidance: Practice and Problems*, 3-17. London: Edward Arnold

Chapter 2

Careers Education in the 20th Century: from 1987

The previous chapter traced the development of careers education in schools over a 30-year period, from its beginnings in the 1960s to the position it occupied in the late 1980s, where, in most schools, careers education featured in the curriculum for all pupils in their final three years of compulsory education. As reported in the conclusion of that chapter, however, towards the end of the 1980s the school curriculum in England was about to undergo its most significant change since the end of the Second World War and the Education Act 1944. In 1987 the government published proposals to introduce a national curriculum and, for the first time in the nation's history, to legislate for the subjects to be included in the curriculum. In the original consultation document careers education was omitted from the list of proposed subjects. This chapter tells the story of how careers education recovered from this situation during the ensuing ten years, culminating in the Education Act 1997 which made careers education a statutory part of the curriculum in secondary schools.

Careers education as a cross-curricular theme

The government's proposals set out ten foundation subjects that should be followed by all pupils aged 5 to 16: three core subjects – English, mathematics and science – and seven other foundation subjects – technology[4], a modern foreign language[5], history, geography, art, music and physical education (DES and Welsh Office, 1987). Although there was no intention to prescribe in legislation how much time should be allocated to each subject, there was an expectation that in secondary schools the core and other foundation subjects should commonly take up 80-90% of the curriculum. Some of the remaining time would have to be given to religious education, the only subject required by statute prior to 1987, so there was precious little time left for other 'non-compulsory' subjects, (e.g. drama, business studies, etc.) never mind other aspects of the curriculum that schools regarded as important such as health education, economic understanding, environmental education and, of course, careers education.

Naturally careers teachers, careers officers and local authority advisers were concerned about the omission of careers education from the proposed National Curriculum and lobbied the

---

4 Later separated into design technology and information technology.
5 Secondary schools only.

government through their professional associations such as the National Association of Careers and Guidance Teachers[6] (NACGT), the Institute of Careers Officers[7] (ICO) and the London and South East Advisers for Careers Education[8]. Schools and employer organisations also made strong representations for the inclusion of careers education in the curriculum. In November 1987 the government introduced the Education Reform Bill and in December published a booklet summarising the proposals and responding to questions and comments received following the consultation (DES, 1987). Careers education was now mentioned as one example of an important theme that would have a key place in the programmes of study for the core and foundation subjects. It was further suggested that what pupils learned through this cross-curricular approach could be brought together and consolidated in the time available outside the National Curriculum. This was at least consistent with the reference in the original consultation document that there were a number of subjects or themes which could be taught through other subjects. Careers teachers and others at the time, however, were concerned that not all subject teachers, struggling to accommodate all the requirements set out in their programmes of study, would be able also to accommodate additional content for careers education and other themes. Furthermore, they had concerns about whether there would in practice be any time available outside the National Curriculum to draw together the various elements of careers education taught through the foundation subjects, and they were not reassured by the phrase, in the original consultation document, that such themes as careers education could be "accommodated within the curriculum but without crowding out the *essential* [my italics] subjects" (op.cit., p.8).

By the time the Education Reform Act 1988 was passed there was a recognition that careers education should be included in the whole curriculum for all pupils but it was not going to be separately identified as part of the statutory National Curriculum (DES, 1989). The argument was put forward that schools would not be able to fulfill the requirements of Section 1 of the Education Reform Act without including careers education in the curriculum. Section 1 entitled every pupil in maintained schools to

6 Later to become the Association for Careers Education and Guidance (ACEG), which eventually merged with other careers professional associations to form the Career Development Institute (CDI).
7 Later to become the Institute of Career Guidance (ICG), another of the professional associations from which the CDI was established.
8 Later to become the Advisers and Inspectors of Careers Education (AICE), which has since disbanded.

a curriculum which:
"(a) promotes the spiritual, moral, cultural, mental and physical development of pupils;
 (b) prepares pupils for the opportunities, responsibilities and experiences of adult life."

HM Inspectorate picked up this theme in the introduction to its paper on careers education and guidance published in the same year as the Education Reform Act (HMI/DES, 1988). Following its original booklet on the curriculum 5 to 16, in 1985, HMI had published several papers, in the *Curriculum Matters* series, on different subject areas. *Curriculum Matters 10* focused on careers education and guidance. It was around this time that the terminology became potentially confusing. Previously the terms 'careers education' and 'careers guidance' had largely been used separately to describe, respectively, *'curriculum programmes to help pupils develop the knowledge and skills to make decisions and transitions'* and *'activities to help pupils as individuals to make choices which are appropriate for them'.* By the time the National Curriculum was being debated it had become commonplace to use the single phrase 'careers education and guidance' to describe both the work in the curriculum and the one-to-one activities. This in turn led to subsequent discussion about the differences, and inter-relationship, between the two principal components. While more recently attempts have been made to be clearer in the use of language, confusion still persists between different people's understanding of careers education and careers guidance, and this presents an additional challenge to practitioners trying to secure provision for careers education in the curriculum.

The HMI paper set out four aims of careers education and guidance:

" to help pupils
- to develop knowledge and understanding of themselves and others as individuals;
- to develop knowledge and understanding of the world in which they live and the employment and other career opportunities that are available;
- to learn how to make considered choices in relation to anticipated careers and occupations;
- to manage the transitions from school to a full and working life effectively." (p.3)

The influence of Law and Watts's (1977) work on the DOTS framework is clear to see. The paper then went on to set out more detailed objectives for both the 5-13 and 13-16 age ranges. The emphasis was still largely on careers education in the final three years of compulsory schooling, but with a recognition of the preparatory work that could be included in the curriculum for the earlier years of secondary education and in primary schools. Further guidance was offered on the role of the careers teacher, or careers co-ordinator, and on the in-service training they should receive. The issue of curriculum organisation was, however, largely avoided. The introductory section said that contributions to careers education and guidance were made in the teaching of many subjects, and in pastoral provision and extra-curricular activities, and then went on to state that careers education and guidance might also be offered through: designated careers lessons; modules within personal and social education; pre-vocational courses; an organised tutorial programme. In a later section possible contributions of various subjects were discussed further but no guidance was offered on the advantages and disadvantages of different models for organising careers education in the curriculum. Perhaps this is understandable at a time when the DES was advocating a cross-curricular approach: while HMI was independent of government, it was the DES that published the *Curriculum Matters* series.

The Education Reform Act established the National Curriculum Council (NCC) as an advisory body to keep the curriculum under review and to publish information and guidance on the school curriculum. The final position of careers education in the first version of the National Curriculum in England was confirmed in the third of the NCC's Curriculum Guidance series (NCC, 1990a). *NCC Curriculum Guidance 3* provided information and guidance on the whole curriculum and identified careers education and guidance as one of five cross-curricular themes seen as essential parts of the whole curriculum. In these early days of the National Curriculum the emphasis was focused heavily on traditional, 'academic' subjects: it was not easy to keep other areas of the curriculum on the agenda. It is said that careers education would not have been included, even as a cross-curricular theme, had it not been for pressure from employer representatives on the NCC's working groups, in particular the Confederation of British Industry (CBI) and the Engineering Employers' Federation. The guidance acknowledged that it would not necessarily be taught entirely through other subjects. Five different approaches to timetabling the cross-curricular themes were offered, with a recognition that schools might well use different combinations of these approaches in different key stages.

The five approaches listed were:

- taught through national curriculum and other subjects
- whole curriculum planning leading to blocks of activities (often referred to as the topic-based, or project-based, approach)
- separately timetabled themes (i.e. discrete lessons)
- taught through separately timetabled PSE
- long-block timetabling (now referred to as 'curriculum days/ weeks').

In the early 1990s, once work started on implementing the National Curriculum in practice, debate about models of curriculum organisation for careers education continued. This is examined in the next section, and then explored further in Chapter 5.

Curriculum models for careers education

Later in 1990 the NCC published guidance on each of the five cross-curricular themes. *Curriculum Guidance 6* (NCC, 1990b) was on careers education and guidance. It started with the by now familiar four aims:

"Careers education and guidance should help pupils to:

- know themselves better
- be aware of education, training and careers opportunities
- make choices about their own continuing education and training, and about career paths
- manage transitions to new roles and situations." (p.2)

However, when setting out more detailed aims, objectives and examples of activities the document did not use this four-part framework. It referred instead to five strands: self; roles; work; career; transition. Fortunately, careers teachers and co-ordinators were able to recognise some correlation with the more established framework and so were able to use the guidance to review and plan their programmes in the new context of the National Curriculum. In another sense the NCC guidance represented a development on from the HMI booklet published two years previously in that it did not concentrate predominately on the older age range; it also provided detailed suggestions about careers education aims and activities in key stages 1, 2 and 3.

With regard to the question of ways of organising careers education and guidance in the curriculum, *NCC Curriculum*

Guidance 6 offered five approaches but not exactly the same five that appeared in the early guidance on the whole curriculum. 'Taught through national curriculum and other subjects' remained but was expressed as 'permeating the whole curriculum'. 'Taught through separately timetabled PSE', ' as a separately timetabled subject' and 'long-block timetabling' were also retained but 'blocks of activities' was dropped and a new approach, added – 'as part of a tutorial programme' – in response to the work of the National Association for Pastoral Care in Education (NAPCE) and others to develop structured programmes of tutorial work as a means of teaching PSE. This section of the NCC booklet provided a useful checklist of pros and cons of each model, to help schools think about which approach or, more likely, combination of approaches to adopt.

At the time of writing this book there is still an ongoing debate about how best to organise careers education in the curriculum, and this is examined in Chapter 5, but it is worth reviewing the issues that were being considered thirty or so years ago. Despite the acknowledgement that the so-called cross-curricular themes did not, necessarily, have to be delivered in a, literally, cross-curricular way, much of the discussion at the time focused on this particular approach. This was mainly because careers co-ordinators feared that they would be pushed in this direction by curriculum managers in the schools, as there would be no time available for discrete careers lessons once the timetable had been filled with national curriculum core and other foundation subjects. Their concerns, justifiably, were, firstly, that not all departments or teachers would be keen to teach elements of careers education in their subject lessons and, secondly, that not all aspects of careers education could be taught through the national curriculum subjects. Thus, while it was recognised that some subjects could readily contribute to the teaching of careers education (probably the most frequently cited example was writing CVs in English), most schools adopted the approach of finding some discrete time for careers education, sometimes enhanced by work planned in the schemes of work for some, but not all, foundation subjects.

The debate then progressed on which approach to take for the discrete element. During the 1960s and 1970s, where careers education appeared in the curriculum it was usually timetabled as separate lessons but, during the 1980s, schools added more and more subjects and themes to the curriculum and there was no longer enough timetable time to allocate careers education a separate lesson each week. Instead schools organised careers education as part of a wider personal and social education (PSE) course or a tutorial programme. But with regard to this approach the models listed in both the *NCC Curriculum Guidance 3* and *NCC Curriculum Guidance 6* do not adequately describe the full range of models. Firstly, we need to distinguish the tutorial programme from a PSE course, although confusingly sometimes the former is referred to as 'PSE time'. The key difference is that a tutorial programme is taught by the form tutors while a PSE course is taught by a team of PSE teachers. The teachers of a PSE course might be specialists in PSE but they could just as likely be a team put together simply because they have time available on their timetables. It becomes important also to distinguish between two types of PSE course: the 'carousel of modules' approach, where different teachers teach their particular elements and the pupils move from one module to another each half-term or term, and the 'integrated course' approach where each teacher teaches the full year's PSE course to her or his class group. This gives a total of six approaches to curriculum organisation:

- separately timetabled careers lessons
- careers education as a module within a modular PSE programme
- careers education as an integrated part of a PSE course
- careers education as part of a tutorial programme
- long-block timetabling
- cross-curricular approach.

In the early 1990s few secondary schools had kept the separate careers lessons model. Some experimented with the cross curricular approach but most organised careers education as part of a PSE or tutorial programme, although a few started to use curriculum days instead. The modular PSE course has the advantage that specialist teachers can teach the careers education component, but this may not be at the most appropriate time in the school year for each group. The tutorial approach enables close links to be established between the careers education lessons and the guidance provided by tutors, but not all tutors are confident and willing to teach careers education. The curriculum days can add value to a careers education programme but are insufficient on their own: a pupil only has to have a dental appointment and he or she would miss their careers education for the year. The approach that has the most advantages, and least disadvantages, is the integrated PSE course but only if it is taught by a small team of teachers who are competent with teaching PSE and not by whichever members of staff are left once the subject timetable has been written. As indicated earlier, the subject of curriculum organisation has been a recurring theme throughout the history of careers education and will be revisited in a later chapter.

Careers Service support for careers education

As the earlier sections of this chapter have described, the early 1990s represented a time when careers education was at risk of being marginalised in a new National Curriculum dominated by traditional academic subjects. One of the factors that helped to ensure that careers education survived in the school curriculum during this period was that local education authorities (LEAs) were still involved in the TVEI extension programme described in the previous chapter. This curriculum development programme, led by the Employment Department, continued to provide funding and support for careers education and guidance in schools, through advisers and advisory teachers employed by LEAs, often using TVEI resources to fund these posts, and through the work of curriculum development advisers in the careers service. At the time LEAs still had responsibility for providing the careers service and the TVEI initiative had brought about a closer working relationship between LEA curriculum advisers and development advisers in the careers service. The careers service did not just provide guidance interviews for young people, it also offered support to schools and colleges to help them develop their provision of careers information and careers education, through consultancy and in-service training for careers teachers. LEA careers services also provided resource centres of classroom materials that teachers could visit before committing their money and many offered bulk purchase schemes to enable schools to buy resources, including some of the IT packages that were emerging, at a discounted price.

It was around this time that careers services began to develop quality awards as a means of both recognising and promoting good practice in careers education and guidance in schools, colleges and training providers (Andrews, 2005). Each award consisted of a set of quality standards, often developed by the local careers service working in partnership with representatives from schools, which schools could use to review their policy and practice. Most services also offered the opportunity of accreditation through an external assessment, leading to the presentation of a certificate. The two most widely known quality awards were *Investor in Careers*, developed by Cornwall and Devon Careers Services and run under licence in many other areas and *Career Mark*, a regional award developed by the East Midlands consortium of careers services, but many areas ran their own local award developed solely for their own schools. These quality awards represent the origins of the single, national award that exists today, the *Quality in Careers Standard*, the development of which is described in Chapter 4.

The role of the careers service in careers education and guidance in schools was the subject of a research study by the National Foundation for Educational Research (NFER) in 1995. The report identified three models of interaction between the careers service and schools (Morris, Simkin & Stoney, 1995). The first, the *parallel* model, was characterised by a minimum of interaction between the school and the careers service. Careers education was seen as the preserve of teachers while guidance primarily took the form of a careers service interview. There was little exchange of information between the school and the careers service and the two components ran separately, with no joint planning. In the second, *pyramidal* model the guidance interview was seen as the culmination of the process and the role of careers education was to prepare pupils for this 'event'. In this more widespread model the pupils were better prepared for the interview and the careers service had some input to the careers education curriculum by providing information, support for the careers library and occasional in-service training for school staff. However, the outcomes of the interview were not used to inform the further development of the careers education programme. This only happened in the third, *guidance community* model, in which careers officers were more actively involved in the process of curriculum planning and review and the careers interview was seen not only as part of the process for the pupil but also used by the school to inform future curriculum development.

The NFER report also discussed the potentially confusing use of terminology mentioned earlier in this chapter. The authors referred to the fact that the literature at the time almost exclusively used the term 'careers education and guidance'. They went on to distinguish between 'careers education' and 'careers guidance' and pointed out that, while there was usually a tacit understanding among teachers and careers officers about the difference between the two and, therefore, the tasks involved, there was sometimes an element of conceptual confusion which followed through into practice, leading to a confusion in tasks and responsibilities. They also suggested that in some schools the provision of careers information was confused with careers education. This section of the report was a valiant attempt to bring clarity to the use of language but it is a problem that has not gone away, as will be seen in later chapters.

During the first half of the 1990s, while the implementation of the National Curriculum was being led by the DES and managed through LEAs, careers education was being supported by careers services which, although part of the LEA, reported to the Employment Department. This reflected the unique position of careers education policy at national level. Responsibility for curriculum policy in all subjects, with the exception of careers education, resided with the DES but responsibility for careers education policy was located in the Careers Service Branch of the Employment Department. This explains why two major initiatives to support careers work in schools at this time came not from the DES, but the Employment Department. In 1992 the Careers Library Initiative made substantial funding available to schools over a two-year period to improve the provision of careers information for pupils and in most areas this was continued in subsequent years, although at a reduced level. In 1994 the government announced that £87 million would be provided over three years from 1995 to improve the quality of careers education in Years 9 and 10[9].

The careers service itself was not immune from major reforms. From 1974 it had been organised as an LEA service but the Conservative administration of the 1980s and early 1990s was committed to privatising the service. After running 13 'pathfinder' services from 1993, the government oversaw the replacement of LEA careers services with 66 private careers services in the three years from 1994 to 1996. The service was still funded with public money and organisations submitted tenders to run the service in geographical areas designated by the government. Many areas went to partnerships of LEAs and Training and Enterprise Councils (TECs) but several went to private companies such as Careers Management, CfBT, Lifetime Careers and Prospects. The Employment Department issued annually a document entitled *Requirements and Guidance for Providers* which set out the services that the new private companies should provide and these included not only guidance for young people but also curriculum support to schools and training for careers teachers. Thus the support that the careers service had provided for careers education under the auspices of the LEAs continued under the new arrangements.

Better Choices

This chapter started by referring to the sudden change in fortunes for careers education when the original proposals for the National Curriculum omitted any reference to careers education, only three months after the same government had published a statement of how important it was. Although the

---

9 The National Curriculum brought about a change in labelling of the year groups in schools. In secondary schools, the third and fourth years became, respectively, Years 9 and 10.

position improved slightly over the next few years, with the publication of curriculum guidance by the NCC and support from the Employment Department and the careers service, there were calls for a clear statement from government, reaffirming the position of careers education and guidance. Such a statement came eventually in 1994 when the Department for Education[10] (DfE) and the Employment Department published the first in what was to become a nine-part series of *Better Choices* booklets (DfE and ED, 1994). In many respects the document was a restatement of the principles set out in *Working Together For A Better Future* (DES, ED and Welsh Office, 1987) and it even used similar phrasing in the sub-title, 'Working Together to Improve Careers Education and Guidance – The Principles'. But this in itself was reassuring to careers teachers and those working with them. The principles remained broadly similar but the context had changed: some schools had opted out of LEA control to become grant-maintained; colleges of further education had been incorporated; the careers service was being privatised; and, Training and Enterprise Councils had been established to oversee work-based training and to foster partnerships with employers. Over the next five years eight further booklets were to be published, each providing guidance and case studies on different aspects of careers education and guidance.

The Employment Department continued to support the development of careers education in schools and in 1995, when the DfE merged with the Employment Department to form the Department for Education and Employment (DfEE), the policy teams from the two departments were integrated into a single Division which could provide coherent direction to the work of both the careers service and schools.

Joined-up support

The DfEE continued to publish guidance in the *Better Choices* series throughout the latter half of the 1990s. It backed this up with an investment in in-service training (INSET) for careers education and guidance. In the period 1995-98 teachers in schools had access to a range of staff development opportunities funded through two sources. The Grant for Education Support and Training (GEST) budgets allocated to LEAs included a specific category for careers education and guidance and the budgets for careers services included funding for INSET. Many LEAs continued the good practice established in the TVEI years of advisers

---

10 Following a re-organisation of government departments in 1992 the DES changed to the DfE

and careers service development officers working together to make best use of the two budgets to provide complementary programmes of training opportunities.

This was the first time since the HMI-led courses in the 1960s that the government had committed significant resources to the training of teachers involved in careers education and guidance. Many survey reports and guidance documents had called for training for careers teachers but it had been left to LEAs and higher education institutions to develop courses. *Working Together For A Better Future* had pointed out the need for in-service training for careers teachers and this did result in the production of an open-learning resource pack *Careers Work* (DES, 1990). The pack was handed over to the Open College and while it was taken up by some LEAs and careers services, and used by both Canterbury Christ Church University and Manchester Metropolitan University to set up distance-learning courses, sustained use of the materials relied on support networks being established and its more lasting impact has been to influence the design of course materials in several different settings over the thirty years since it was first published.

It was not only the government departments and the careers service that were undergoing changes in organisation at this time. The NCC was replaced in 1993 by the School Curriculum and Assessment Authority (SCAA) and then in 1997 SCAA merged with the National Council for Vocational Qualifications (NCVQ) to form the Qualifications and Curriculum Authority (QCA). Both new curriculum bodies published guidelines on careers education. In 1995 SCAA produced *Looking Forward* (SCAA, 1995), with the intention of bringing up to date the NCC's 1990 publication and complementing the *Better Choices* booklets. *Looking Forward* represented a move on from *NCC Curriculum Guidance 6* in two important respects. Firstly, the booklet included suggestions for careers education in post-16 education as well as for key stages 1 to 4. Secondly, it reframed the aims of careers education while remaining consistent with the DOTS framework. The five strands that were introduced in *NCC Curriculum Guidance 6* were ignored; instead the guidelines set out three broad aims for programmes of careers education and guidance:

1. Understand themselves and develop their capabilities.
2. Investigate careers and opportunities.
3. Implement their career plans.

Each aim was a development of one or more of the 'DOTS' aims. Aim 1 moved on from 'self awareness' and implied that pupils should not just get to know themselves better, but should take action to develop themselves. Similarly, Aim 2 moved on from 'opportunity awareness' and encouraged schools to think about how to enable pupils to research careers information themselves rather than just be given a series of careers talks. Aim 3 combined 'decision learning' and 'transition-learning' into taking action to use the skills to make choices and transitions. The intention was to promote more active and participative approaches to teaching and learning in careers lessons.

Career learning theory

The DOTS framework established by Law and Watts (op cit.) continued to influence the design of careers education programmes in schools, and the structure of official guidelines on this area of the curriculum, throughout the 1980s and 1990s and, as we shall see in the next chapter, into the next century. Almost 20 years after this simple but enduring conceptualisation of careers education was first published one of its authors Bill Law (in Watts, Law, Killeen, Kidd and Hawthorn, 1996) set out his ideas for a career learning theory that built on the DOTS framework but added the notion of progression in learning. Law argued that the DOTS framework was useful in helping to determine what careers education programmes should cover, in terms of curriculum content, but that it was limited in its use as a planning tool as it did not inform decisions about the order in which the content should be sequenced. He drew upon the concept of progression in learning to propose a model that set out stages in learning about self, opportunities, decisions and transitions.

Each of the four main stages was divided into two sub-stages to give a total of eight steps in learning, from the basic and simple to the highly advanced and complex. Law suggested that one of the problems for careers education in schools is that all too often we ask pupils to deal with quite challenging questions and to grasp sophisticated ideas before we have helped them to acquire more basic knowledge, understanding and skills. In his training workshops he would say that we ask young people to make career choices before they have enough to go on. He used the idea of progression to show how careers learning should move from gathering information to taking action: the various steps set out below were to help careers teachers to sequence the activities in their programmes of careers education so that prior learning led to subsequent learning.

Figure 2. Progression in career learning (from Law, in Watts, Law, Killeen, Kidd and Hawthorn, 1996)

Sensing
- gathering information
- assembling sequences

Sifting
- making comparisons
- using concepts

Focusing
- appreciating different points of view
- taking one's own view

Understanding
- developing explanations
- anticipating consequences

DES Survey 18 had referred to careers education being implemented in two stages – a divergent phase of exploration and a convergent phase of decision-making (DES, 1973). Law's career learning theory developed this basic idea into a planning framework. The DOTS framework and the Sensing, Sifting, Focusing, Understanding (SSFU) framework could be combined into a two-dimensional matrix, with one axis helping schools to determine the content of a careers education programme and the other to assist with placing the activities and ideas into an appropriate order. Evidence to date shows that although later guidelines for careers education from the government and its advisory bodies attempted to include elements of progression in the objectives and activities suggested, none of them made explicit use of career learning theory. The impact of the SSFU framework has been greater on practice in individual schools that have participated in workshops using the ideas set out in the theory.

A place in the statutory curriculum

This chapter has described how, through the 1990s, careers education survived its omission from the original proposals for the National Curriculum, and continued to develop in schools through support from government, and its advisory bodies, LEAs and the careers service. However, its position in the school curriculum was still relatively weak - an optional, cross-curricular theme outside the National Curriculum. Despite lobbying from the professional associations the government appeared unlikely to change the status of careers education, but then, towards the end of the decade and in what turned out to be the last Education Act of the Conservative government, there was a positive move to strengthen the position. Heavily influential in the decision were employers and, in particular, the CBI. As suggested in the previous chapter it has been argued that the origins of the National Curriculum can be traced back to Prime Minister Jim Callaghan's speech in 1976 and the 'Great Debate' that followed. Throughout its work on introducing the National Curriculum the government had listened to the views of the business world. The CBI had called for the weak position of careers education and guidance in schools as a cross-curricular theme to be transformed and had recommended that the government should define and support the entitlement to careers education for 14-16 year-olds (CBI, 1993). In the Education Act 1997 the government set out new statutory requirements for careers education and guidance. Section 43 placed a statutory duty on schools to provide a programme of careers education in the curriculum for all pupils in Years 9, 10 and 11, with effect from September 1998. This was regarded as minimalist legislation as it only required all schools to do what most schools already did, but it was considered an important milestone in that for the first time careers education would be part of the statutory curriculum. Furthermore the legislation was drafted in such a way that the government could at a later date amend the duty without having to pass primary legislation – a power that the Labour government was to use to good effect a few years later to extend the duty to include all pupils in Years 7 and 8. That, however, was not the last occasion on which the duty was changed: in 2012 the Conservative and Liberal Democrat Coalition government removed the duty completely, thereby putting into reverse half a century of progress. The need to rebuild the position of careers education in the curriculum is the main motivation behind writing this second edition.

In 1997 SCAA had been replaced by QCA and in 1999 the new curriculum authority published guidance to help schools to plan the programme of careers education required by the new legislation (QCA, 1999). The QCA document used the same three aims set out in the SCAA document four years previously, although now abbreviated to 'self development', 'careers exploration' and 'career management'. It retained a section for post-16 education but dropped sections on the two primary school key stages. The last in the *Better Choices* series provided advice to schools and careers services on developing the careers education curriculum in schools (DfEE, 1999a). So, by the end of the decade that started with careers education being at risk of being squeezed out of the curriculum, it had been made a statutory requirement, supported by curriculum guidance and training. Although the GEST funding given to LEAs for careers teacher training ended in 1998, the careers service continued to support in-service training. In 1999 the DfEE funded CAMPAG, the national organisation for education, training and standards in Advice, Guidance and Counselling, to develop National Occupational Standards for Careers Education and Guidance in Schools and Colleges (DfEE, 1999b) which were to be used later as a basis for developing a National Vocational Qualification (NVQ) in co-ordinating careers education and guidance.

DfEE gave out a very strong signal about the importance it placed on careers education in schools by appointing to the role of Chief Inspector of Careers Services a former headteacher, Graham Robb. Previously holders of this senior post had always been recruited from careers services.

End of the century surveys

Towards the end of the 1990s two surveys of careers education and guidance in schools were published, one a national survey of careers education and guidance in secondary schools undertaken by Ofsted (1998), the other a survey of careers education and guidance in British schools undertaken by the NACGT (1999).

The Ofsted survey found that the attainment of pupils was satisfactory in about 70% of schools, the quality of teaching was satisfactory in eight out of ten careers lessons and the leadership and management of careers education and guidance were satisfactory in 75% of schools. However, Ofsted also reported that a quarter of schools did not offer a planned and well organised programme of careers education. The report stated that the wide variation in both the content and the time allocated for careers education was unacceptable. 10% of schools allowed no more than three hours of careers teaching in Year 10 and 11, while in contrast 20% allocated more than 20 hours to the same year groups. The survey found that one in two teachers of careers had a very good understanding of careers education and guidance, but the other half were insufficiently trained. While the GEST funding had had a positive impact in two-thirds of schools, only one in three careers co-ordinators held a recognised careers qualification. Overall the findings suggested that since the NACGT survey of 1986, there had been an increase in training for careers teachers but a major issue remained the time allocated to careers education in the curriculum. The trend to organise careers education as part of a programme of PSE had continued, with this being the model adopted by 70% of schools at the time of the Ofsted survey. However the report indicated that the most commonly used approach was a poorly designed rotational system where, in the worst cases, students were having to study how to apply for jobs and college places one and a half years before the earliest school leaving date. The survey found that relationships between schools and careers services were good but the main contribution careers advisers[11] were making remained the guidance interview; they had little influence on the design and content of careers education programmes. The careers library initiative had led to an improvement in most schools but in a quarter the range and quality of careers information on offer was poor. The Year 9 and Year 10 initiative has made a positive impact in nearly half of schools, and increased the amount of teaching time allocated to careers education in Year 9.

The NACGT survey reported a slightly more positive picture. For example, it found that 42% of careers co-ordinators held, or were working towards, a professional qualification. The courses most frequently mentioned were those at the Cambridge Institute of Education, Canterbury Christ Church University, Manchester Metropolitan University and Nottingham Trent University. With regard to time allocations for careers education in the curriculum, the survey reported the following averages per year:

Years 7 & 8	6-7 hours
Year 9	13-14 hours
Years 10 & 11	20-22 hours
Years 12 & 13	14-17 hours.

The survey also found that nearly half of schools had achieved, or were working towards, a quality award.

By the end of the 20th century careers education had secured a place in the statutory curriculum but the quality of provision varied from school to school. Further work would be required before we could be assured that all pupils had access to the support they needed if they were to plan and manage their careers successfully in the next century.

---

11 Following the privatisation of the careers service most companies used the term careers adviser instead of the former job title of careers officer.

References

Andrews, D. (2005). *Quality Awards for CEG in England: a survey of current availability and uptake.* Cambridge: NICEC

Confederation of British Industry (1993). *Routes for success.* London: CBI

Department for Education and Employment Department (1994). *Better Choices.* London: DfE & ED

Department for Education and Employment (1999a). *Better Choices. Developing the Careers Education Curriculum in Schools.* London: DfEE

Department for Education and Employment (1999b). *National Occupational Standards for Careers Education and Guidance in Schools and Colleges.* London: DfEE

Department of Education and Science (1973). *Survey 18 Careers Education in Secondary Schools.* London: HMSO

Department of Education and Science (1987). *Education Reform. The Government's Proposals for Schools.* London: DES

Department of Education and Science (1989). *National Curriculum: from Policy to Practice.* London: DES

Department of Education and Science (1990). *Careers Work.* London: DES

Department of Education and Science, Department of Employment and Welsh Office (1987). *Working Together For A Better Future.* London: Central Information Office

Department of Education and Science and Welsh Office (1987). *The National Curriculum 5-16: a consultation document.* London: DES

Her Majesty's Inspectorate/Department of Education and Science (1988). *Careers education and guidance from 5 to 16. Curriculum Matters 10.* London: HMSO

Law, B. (1996). A career learning theory. In Watts, A.G., Law, B., Killeen, J., Kidd, J.M. and Hawthorn, R. (eds) *Rethinking Careers Education and Guidance*, 46-71. London: Routledge

Law, B and Watts, A. G. (1977). *Schools, Careers and Community.* London: Church Information Office

Morris, M., Simkin, C. and Stoney, S. (1995). *The Role of the Careers Service in Careers Education and Guidance in Schools.* Sheffield: Employment Department

National Association of Careers and Guidance Teachers (1999). *1999 Survey of Careers Education and Guidance in British Schools.* London: NACGT

National Curriculum Council (1990a). *Curriculum Guidance 3: The Whole Curriculum.* York: NCC

National Curriculum Council (1990b). *Curriculum Guidance 6: Careers Education and Guidance.* York: NCC

Office for Standards in Education (1998). *National Survey of Careers Education and Guidance (Secondary Schools).* London: Ofsted

Qualifications and Curriculum Authority (1999). *Learning outcomes from careers education and guidance.* London: QCA

School Curriculum and Assessment Authority (1995). *Looking Forward: Careers Education and Guidance in the Curriculum.* London: SCAA

Chapter 3

Careers education in the 21st Century: the first ten years

At the turn of the century the position of careers education in the school curriculum in England was stronger than it had been at any time in its brief history. Over the next few years however, this position was to be threatened by two major policy initiatives: firstly, further reforms to the curriculum; and, secondly, the replacement of careers services with Connexions partnerships. This chapter examines the impact of these two developments on careers education policy and practice throughout the first decade of the new century. It is a story of how careers education in schools retained its place in the curriculum but, at the same time, remained vulnerable to the influence of wider policy changes. Even at the end of the decade, when it could be argued that careers education enjoyed an even stronger position than it did at the beginning, it was not secure, as we will see in the chapter that follows this.

The revised National Curriculum

By the beginning of the new millennium the National Curriculum had been in place for just over ten years. During this period there had been a growing consensus of support for a national entitlement to a common curriculum but throughout concerns had been expressed that the requirements were too prescriptive, in terms of both the amount of content in each subject and the number of different subjects to be studied in key stage 4. In response the government had changed the statutory position of some subjects so that, firstly, art and music and, later, history and geography became optional at key stage 4. Then, from 1998, schools were permitted to disapply some pupils from the requirements to study two of the three subjects design technology, a modern foreign language and science at key stage 4, in order to follow a programme of work-related learning. In 2000 the entire National Curriculum was revised with the principal objective of reducing the level of prescription. However, the New Labour government took this opportunity to add a new subject to the list of foundation subjects to be studied in secondary schools: from 2002, schools were to be required to include citizenship in the curriculum for all pupils in key stages 3 and 4.

In 2000 careers education benefited from a strong position in terms of policy. It was a statutory requirement in Years 9, 10 and 11, supported by a framework of learning outcomes published by QCA (1999) and curriculum advice and in-service training from the privatised careers service. In terms of practice, the amount of time allocated to careers education and the quality of provision varied across schools (Ofsted, 1998). There was a recognition that, while many schools had good programmes, more work needed to be done to bring all schools up to the standard of the best and to ensure that all pupils in all schools received good quality careers education. The 2000 revision to the National Curriculum presented both an opportunity and a challenge to the further development of careers education in schools. The reduction in prescription meant that there would be more time available for schools to devote to aspects that were positioned outside the national curriculum foundation subjects, particularly statutory elements such as careers education[12]. At the same time there was a very real risk that the limited time available for careers education could be squeezed further by the need to find time in the timetable for the new subject citizenship, particularly as this was designated a national curriculum foundation subject, a status that had never been granted to careers education.

To help schools turn this potential threat into an opportunity the DfEE (2000a) published a booklet showing the links between the learning outcomes for careers education at key stages 3 and 4, and both the framework for personal, social and health education (PSHE) and the programme of study for citizenship. As reported in the previous chapter, in 1995 the education and employment departments had been merged into a single government department but the position of national policy responsibility for careers education remained separate from that for all other aspects of the curriculum. The Curriculum Division, based in London, had responsibility for all aspects of the curriculum except careers education, responsibility for which remained with the Choice and Information Division, that had oversight of the careers service and which was based in Sheffield. The Choice and Information Division took advantage of this situation to publish several guidance booklets, all aimed at strengthening the position of careers education in schools. In addition to the curriculum guidance mentioned above, the Department for Education and Employment (DfEE) published a guide to help governors and senior managers to understand and manage careers education and guidance in schools (DfEE, 2000b) and a booklet demonstrating how good quality careers work could contribute to school improvement (DfEE, 2000c). To this day some

---

[12] The statutory components of the school curriculum at the time comprised: the national curriculum core and other foundation subjects; RE; and, in secondary schools, sex education and, in years 9, 10 and 11, careers education.

senior leaders in schools argue that they cannot give priority to careers education and guidance because such activities divert time away from the study of GCSE subjects and run the risk of the school not achieving as many high grade passes as they might, while research (e.g. Killeen, Sammons and Watts, 1999; Hooley, Matheson and Watts, 2014) shows precisely the opposite, that careers education and guidance has positive effects on academic attainment. The Choice and Information Division also published guidance (DfEE, 2001) on what it referred to as 'career-related learning' in primary schools, showing how careers education activities in key stages 1 and 2 could lay the foundations for careers education and guidance in secondary schools, an issue the government was to re-visit a few years later.

Government support for careers education in schools at this time extended beyond the publication of guidelines. Careers education programmes were quite well established in the curriculum for years 9, 10 and 11 but not so prominent in the first two years of key stage 3. In the late 1990s interest grew in a resource developed originally in Canada, *The Real Game* (Edwards, Barnes, Killeen and Watts, 1999), and in 2000 the DfEE launched the first UK version of the pack. *The Real Game* aimed to help pupils in Years 8 and 9 explore careers and the world of work in an enjoyable, relevant and meaningful way before they would be asked later in Year 9 to make an important choice of subjects to be studied from age 14. A year later, in 2001, the government made a major investment by launching the Careers Education Support Programme. The DfEE commissioned a partnership of Careers Management (a private careers guidance company) and the NACGT (the professional association for careers teachers) to manage and deliver the programme. At its heart was a website (www.cegnet.co.uk) which was to become the first port of call for anyone interested in planning and developing careers education in schools. The government funded the programme from 2001 to 2010 and throughout this period the website continued to provide regular updates and access to downloadable resources.

National Framework for CEG

In the world of careers education and guidance the early years of this decade are probably best remembered for the publication of the national framework for careers education and guidance 11-19 (DfES, 2003a)[13]. The guidelines presented a national, non-statutory framework of recommended learning outcomes for careers education in key stages 3 and 4, and in post-16 education and training. The framework built on the previous guidance provided by QCA and, before that, SCAA, and was organised around the same three aims that had been used in those earlier guidelines, i.e. that young people should be able to:

- understand themselves and the influences on them (self development)
- investigate opportunities in learning and work (career exploration)
- make and adjust plans to manage change and transition (career management).

There were no sections on careers education in key stages 1 and 2, but the post-16 section was more substantial than the equivalent section in the previous guidelines. Use of the new framework was promoted by careers education advisers working in local education authorities, careers companies and the new Connexions partnerships (see next section) who ran conferences to raise awareness and courses and workshops to support the implementation of the framework in practice.

QCA had been slightly hesitant in supporting publication of the new guidelines on careers education because of its own plans to publish guidance on work-related learning at key stage 4, following the government's decision, in 2003, to make work-related learning a statutory requirement in the curriculum for 14-16 year old pupils with effect from September 2004. Nevertheless, the DfES went ahead with its plans and when the guidance on work-related learning at key stage 4 was published the framework included two elements that could be clearly identified as careers education (QCA, 2004). Schools were able to use the two booklets alongside each other to plan a coherent provision of both careers education and work-related learning in the curriculum for key stage 4, where the links could be reinforced

---

13 After the 2001 general election, the employment functions of the DfEE were transferred to a newly created Department for Work and Pensions, and the education department was re-named the Department for Education and Skills.

and the risk of duplication avoided. One of the more obvious links between careers education and work-related learning was work experience, which had been a strong feature of the TVEI developments described in the previous chapter. During the period covered by the present chapter the vast majority of schools included a period of work experience on employers' premises as an integral part of the careers education programme for all pupils aged 14 to 16. The new statutory duty and accompanying guidelines stimulated schools to go further and to develop other elements of work-related learning, in particular enterprise activities for which, at the time, schools received additional funding.

Simultaneous to publishing the careers education framework the government used a power established by the Education Act 1997 to extend, by regulation, the age range to which the duty on schools to provide careers education applied. With effect from September 2004, schools were required to teach careers education in Years 7 and 8, as well as in Years 9, 10 and 11. The government had recently published its proposals to reform 14-19 education and training (DfES, 2003b). If pupils were to make informed choices in Year 9 about the courses and programmes they would follow in the 14-19 phase, starting their programmes of careers education at the statutory minimum of Year 9 would be too late. This was particularly true in those schools that had opted to restructure the curriculum into a two-year key stage 3 and a three-year key stage 4, in order to give pupils more time to study their GCSE subjects and with the aim of boosting their position in the performance tables. Pupils would need to start to gain knowledge and understanding of themselves and the opportunities ahead at an earlier stage.

It was for these reasons that the framework for careers education and guidance started at age 11 and the statutory duty to teach careers education was extended to cover the age range 11 to 16. One consequence of this was that, in those LEAs that had retained a three-tier structure of school organisation[14], the statutory duty to teach careers education now applied to middle schools. Secondary schools and middle schools had to review the careers education provided in Years 7 and 8. There was no expectation that the curriculum in these years would include as many hours of careers education as were allocated in Year 9, or that it had to be labeled careers education, but schools were encouraged to use the key stage 3 sections of the framework to review and plan what work they included in the 11-14 curriculum to help pupils develop

---

14 First schools (5-9), middle schools (9-13) and upper schools (13-19).

themselves, explore careers and acquire the skills to make plans and transitions.

Connexions

Alongside reforms to the curriculum the other major policy change that impacted significantly on careers work in schools at the beginning of the new century was the radical reform of guidance services for young people. In 1997 the Conservative administration, which had been in office for 18 years, was replaced by New Labour. The new government was committed to tackling the problems of social exclusion and in 2000 announced its plans to establish a new youth support service (DfEE, 2000d). The proposed Connexions service would subsume the responsibilities of the careers service and work closely with the youth service, social services, health authorities and other organisations to provide integrated guidance and support to young people. The service was organised as 47 Connexions partnerships working under the direction of the Connexions Service National Unit (CSNU) based within the DfEE, and introduced in two phases from April 2001. To demonstrate that the service was different from that which had existed previously the local partnerships were all required to use the Connexions brand with its distinctive purple and gold logo, and all the staff that provided frontline services to young people were henceforth to be called personal advisers.

From the outset the intention was that Connexions would provide coherent support services to all young people, but there was a strong emphasis on helping more vulnerable individuals, in particular those who had dropped out of education or who were at significant risk of becoming disengaged or disaffected. While schools welcomed this attention to joined up services and to supporting those in greatest need, there was a concern that this might result in a reduced careers guidance service for the large majority of pupils. This issue became characterised as a debate about the balance between a universal service (usually regarded as careers guidance for all young people) and a targeted service (i.e. more intensive support, from a range of services, for the significant minority of young people experiencing a number of personal and social problems). The DfEE itself referred to Connexions offering both a universal advice and guidance service to all pupils and personal support to those in need (DfEE, 2000e). In fact it was the concern about the level of careers advice and guidance available to pupils from the external service that became the bigger issue for schools rather than any questions about support for careers education. In its guidance to

Connexions partnerships the CSNU (2001) made it clear that "the Connexions service should support schools in delivering careers education by consultancy support on curriculum development and by teacher training" (p.14). It went on to say that "Connexions partnerships hold budgets specifically for this purpose, and should ensure that they have the expertise necessary to support schools in this way" (p.14). Connexions partnerships, therefore, continued to provide the types of support for careers education in schools that had been offered previously by the careers service companies. Often the personnel providing the curriculum support remained the same individuals, working directly for a Connexions partnership or for the careers service company which was now providing services under contract to the Connexions partnership. In many areas of England these advisers for careers education formed regional networks which met at least termly, to share practice and, on occasions, to work collaboratively on projects such as joint in-service training programmes and developing resource materials. In 1998 the author of this book had organised the first national conference for careers education advisers and this continued as an annual event for a further 20 years.

In the early years Connexions maintained the support for careers education so, instead of threatening its position in the curriculum, it reinforced the guidance published by the DfEE. It was only in later years that the level of support for careers education became a concern in some areas of the country, as an unintended outcome of reforms to Connexions. Schools had been right to voice worries over the level of careers guidance provided by Connexions, compared with that which they had enjoyed during the era of the privatised careers services. Operating with fewer resources than originally anticipated, and being held accountable by a headline target to reduce the percentage of young people not in education, employment or training (NEET), meant that inevitably Connexions services focused first on their targeted support and ran the risk that not all young people in need of careers advice received it (NAO, 2004). The National Audit Office report, together with persistent feedback from headteachers, led the DfES to undertake an end-to-end review of careers education and guidance (DfES, 2005). The review concluded that insufficient priority had been given to careers guidance in many Connexions partnerships and the government's response was to propose a re-organisation of Connexions. Responsibility and funding for information, advice and guidance (IAG) for young people was to be devolved from the Connexions partnerships to local authorities who would in turn, work with schools and colleges to commission IAG services for the young people in their area. The rationale behind this change was that local authorities, in consultation with schools and colleges, would be best placed to assess the needs in their area and determine the appropriate balance of universal and targeted support. These plans were confirmed and, implemented from April 2008 (DfES, 2006).

Discussion about whether or not the move to local authorities succeeded in redressing the balance between careers guidance and wider IAG will not be pursued here but we do know that it had a detrimental effect on the support for careers education in a small number of areas. Under the new arrangements for Connexions three models emerged. In some areas the local authority took the Connexions service in-house and directly managed it; in others the local authority contracted with the former Connexions partnership to continue to provide the service; in the remaining areas the local authority contracted with one of the private careers guidance companies (McGowan, Watts and Andrews, 2009). In a few areas, mainly ones in which the service had been taken in-house, the IAG service focused on providing IAG to individuals and the support for developing careers education was no longer part of the service. One of the reasons for this omission could be that, unlike when it first established the Connexions service, the government did not issue a specification of the IAG service that local authorities were required to commission. It had developed quality standards for young people's IAG and these made reference to IAG providers working with schools and colleges or programmes of careers education, but not all local authorities referred to the quality standards in detail when establishing the new arrangements (DCSF, 2007)[15].

Another explanation could be in the term 'IAG'. Although adult guidance services had been called IAG partnerships the term first appeared in relation to services for young people in the *Youth Matters* green paper. It represented an attempt to indicate that the services available to young people should extend beyond help with making decisions about their futures to include support for any issues they may be facing in their teenage years. It did, however, also present a risk that policy makers and those responsible for allocating resources to careers work, both in local authorities and in schools and colleges, might think IAG was limited to, literally, information, advice and guidance, and that work in the curriculum, careers education, could be forgotten. In later years the term was extended to careers education and IAG

---

15 In 2007, a re-organisation of responsibilities across several government departments resulted in the DfES changing its name to the Department for Children, Schools and Families.

(CEIAG), for example when the contract to provide the national support programme was put out to tender again in 2008, it was re-titled the Careers Education and IAG Support Programme.

14-19 and IAG

Throughout the decade the government continued to pursue its programme of reforming 14-19 learning. In 2003 the DfES commissioned a review of 14-19 education and training, under the chairmanship of Mike Tomlinson, a former Chief Inspector of Schools, to build a consensus of the reforms needed to ensure that young people were equipped to succeed in the 21st century. The review proposed replacing existing qualifications with a unified framework of diplomas (DfES, 2004). In the run up to the 2005 general election the government drew back from implementing the Tomlinson proposals in full, partly because they involved dropping both GCSEs and A levels. Instead it selected some of the proposals and introduced a more limited set of reforms, including new applied learning programmes, called Diplomas.

Over the next few years the government then added further elements to the reform programme including revised GCSEs and A levels, enhanced apprenticeships, foundation learning and legislation to raise the age of participation in learning to, firstly 17, and then 18. In many of the reports and guidelines there was a recognition of the critical role of information, advice and guidance (e.g. DCSF, 2008). The reforms provided more flexibility in the curriculum and new qualifications, they also positively encouraged schools and colleges to work collaboratively to increase the range of opportunities available to young people, but they would not work in practice unless young people received the right information, advice and guidance. IAG was seen as being vital to making the system work for young people and, as a result, it started to receive more attention and support. For example, the DfES funded a major support programme to assist 14-19 consortia to implement the new Diplomas and a critical part of the support was a team of regional IAG Champions managed by the Specialist Schools and Academies Trust (SSAT).

The increased attention on IAG culminated in the publication of an IAG strategy which was viewed by several commentators and practitioners as 'putting careers back into IAG' and finally stating the need for a strong careers guidance service as part of a wider range of support for young people (DCSF, 2009a). Publication of the strategy had been delayed for a few months, partly because of a change in the ministerial team within the

DCSF, but mainly as a result of one of the recommendations in the Milburn Report on fair access to the professions, which was published while the IAG strategy was been drafted. The report was quite critical of the careers advice and guidance provided by Connexions and recommended that the government should remove responsibility for careers IAG from Connexions and allocate an estimated £200 million to schools and colleges in order to give them the freedom to tender for careers services from a range of providers (COI, 2009). Before it could publish its new IAG strategy the government had to respond to this criticism and recommendation contained within a report of what was an all-party panel but chaired by one of its own ministers. The final version of the strategy acknowledged the evidence to suggest that the quality of IAG delivered through Connexions was variable but the government decided not to accept the recommendation to give responsibility for careers advice and guidance directly to schools. Instead they promised to formally review the quality and effectiveness of local authorities' delivery of IAG in 18 months to two years' time, i.e. sometime in the middle of 2011. As we shall see in the next chapter, a new government was to return to this issue and take a different view.

The strategy included an IAG guarantee to make explicit the provision that young people and their parents had a right to receive. This was to be embedded within new pupil and parent guarantees covering a wider range of educational provision and to be introduced in legislation planned for 2010. The young people's IAG guarantee included an entitlement to "high quality programmes of careers education which help young people to plan and manage their own careers [and] impartial information, advice and guidance about learning and work options" (p.14). The parent guarantee proposed that "every parent should expect to receive high quality information and advice through school about the career and subject choices open to their child" (p.25). The strategy acknowledged the importance of strengthening the position of careers education alongside improving careers information, advice and guidance, and included several specific actions to improve the quality of careers education in schools and colleges. Alongside the IAG strategy the government published statutory guidance on careers education in schools, which is examined in greater detail in the next section (DCSF, 2009b).

The strategy also stated an ambition to extend the statutory duty to provide careers education up to age 18, an intention to support pilots of careers-related learning in key stage 2 and a commitment to exploring how to develop new qualifications for careers co-ordinators. By the end of 2009 the future of both careers guidance and careers education looked very positive again. Whether that situation prevailed will be examined in the next chapter but before that we need to go back to the end-to-end review of careers education and guidance and track developments in relation to the curriculum dimension.

Careers education: PSHE education and statutory guidance

The end-to-end review of careers education and guidance undertaken in 2004 and published in 2005 had identified a lack of priority given to careers guidance in some Connexions partnerships. This led to the reforms outlined in the previous section and, ultimately, the publication of the IAG strategy. The review also identified a lack of priority given to careers education in schools. At first little action was taken in response to this finding: all the attention was on addressing concerns about careers guidance. In the meantime the DfES worked with QCA to undertake a further review of the secondary curriculum and the new curriculum began in schools in September 2008. Careers education remained a statutory requirement and, in an attempt to promote more integrated approaches to a series of previously separately identified elements of the curriculum, it was presented as one component of personal, social, health and economic (PSHE) education. The term 'PSHE' had been redefined to encompass two strands: personal wellbeing and economic wellbeing. Earlier the DfES had published a vision for children's services *Every Child Matters* which identified five outcomes that all young people should achieve: be healthy; stay safe; enjoy and achieve; make a positive contribution; achieve economic wellbeing (DfES, 2003c). Alongside work-related learning and enterprise and personal finance education, careers education was seen as important in helping pupils achieve the fifth outcome. QCA had developed a new set of aims for the secondary curriculum (QCA, 2007a). "The curriculum should enable all young people to become: successful learners, who enjoy learning, make progress and achieve; confident individuals, who are able to live, safe, healthy and fulfilling lives; responsible citizens, who make a positive contribution to society" (p.6). It is possible to argue that the knowledge, understanding, skills and attitudes that students develop through careers education contribute to all three aims but the link is most obvious in relation to the third aim. One of the main ways in which responsible citizens make a positive contribution to society is through work and careers education helps individuals to transition into work that they both enjoy and find fulfilling.

Further guidance was developed and schools now had three different but inter-related planning and review tools: the 2003 national framework for careers education and guidance 11-19; the new, non-statutory programmes of study for PSHE: economic wellbeing and financial capability for key stages 3 and 4 (QCA, 2007b and 2007c); and, a framework to support economic wellbeing (QCA, 2008).

In 2008 the government strengthened the statutory duty on schools to provide careers education. Schools already had a duty to teach careers education in all years from age 11 to age 16. The Education and Skills Act 2008 placed an additional duty on them to act impartially when providing careers information and careers education. This gave the DCSF an opportunity to issue guidance to support schools in meeting this statutory requirement and, by so doing, take belated action to respond to the end-to-end review finding. The statutory guidance on impartial careers education was different from all previous guidelines in that it represented a deliberate attempt to engage directly with headteachers. The guidance set out a checklist of 12 key points for headteachers to consider in order to establish appropriate leadership and management arrangements for careers education and IAG in the school. It went on to list six principles of impartial careers education, each accompanied by short outcome-focused statements which schools could use to assess the extent to which they were meeting the principles in practice. A later section took the key points for headteachers and offered practical advice on each one. The DCSF took seriously the need to bring school senior leaders on board and, in a related initiative, funded the National College for Leadership of Schools and Children's Services to produce case studies of good practice (National College, 2009).

The DCSF commissioned the CEIAG Support Programme to produce a resources pack to support the implementation of the statutory guidance (DCSF, 2010). The pack was released at the beginning of 2010 and included: briefings for governors, careers co-ordinators and other staff; classroom resources, information leaflets and a DVD; a new framework for careers education 7-19, structured around the six principles but cross-referenced to the three aims of careers education used in the 2003 framework; an audit tool for careers co-ordinators to use to assess if pupils were achieving the outcomes recommended in the framework; a diagnostic tool for senior leaders, based on the checklist of key action points set out in the statutory guidance. Short of supplying a professionally qualified careers co-ordinator, a team of committed and enthusiastic teachers of careers education and an unlimited resources budget, it is difficult to see what else the DCSF could have provided to ensure effective careers education in the nation's schools.

It is worth mentioning how the 2009 careers education framework differed from the one published in 2003. Firstly, it covered the age range 7 to 19, rather than 11-19, reflecting the interest in developing careers-related learning in the later years of primary schools. Secondly, it presented the first serious attempt to reflect in official guidelines, progression in learning in careers education. It did not follow explicitly the sensing, sifting, focusing and understanding model (Law, 1996) but taking the outcome statements from the statutory guidance as the learning outcomes for key stage 4, it tried to identify what the related prior learning outcomes would be at key stages 2 and 3, and the subsequent learning outcomes in the post-16 stage. These two developments were viewed positively by careers co-ordinators when the resources pack was first made available. The third major difference from the 2003 framework was that it was based on the six principles rather than the well-established three aims. Careers co-ordinators took more time to get accustomed to this but were reassured by the cross-referencing to the three aims. A fourth difference should also be noted: the 2010 version was a framework for careers education, distinguishing it from careers guidance.

The previous chapter examined in some depth different approaches to organising careers education in the curriculum. The issue was raised again in the statutory guidance, which guided headteachers away from using form tutors to teach careers education and suggested instead establishing dedicated teams of specialist PSHE education teachers. The guidance also advised against using what it referred to as 'drop-down days' as the sole means of providing careers education. A further challenge to delivering careers education through tutors had emerged. A growing number of schools had reorganised their tutorial groups into what is known as the 'vertical' system, where each tutor group is made up of small numbers of pupils from each year group. This was reported to have benefits in terms of guidance, support and social interaction, but presented real difficulties in terms of teaching a tutorial programme of age-related material such as careers education.

As a further lever to promote and support the development of careers education in schools the statutory guidance included an appendix illustrating how careers education and IAG impacted on the judgements made in Ofsted inspections. From the outset, when Ofsted was established in 1992, there had been concerns that careers education was not given the same attention in the inspection framework as other subjects in the curriculum. Ofsted itself tried to address this by publishing guidance to inspectors and schools on inspecting and evaluating careers education and guidance (Ofsted, 2001), but it was not until the version of the inspection schedule published in 2009 that careers education was referred to explicitly. The framework used at the time of the statutory guidance was published required inspectors to judge "the extent to which pupils develop workplace and other skills that will contribute to their future economic wellbeing" and "the extent to which pupils understand their future options". However, as the process of inspection for the average secondary school consisted of a team of just four inspectors spending two days in the school, there remained concerns about whether all sections of the schedule could be covered in detail. Effective use of the self-evaluation form, which followed the same structure as the inspection framework, was likely to offer greater scope for supporting the development of careers education.

Training for careers co-ordinators

The two previous chapters have referred to surveys over the years calling for more training for careers teachers and careers co-ordinators but decisions about what to offer and in what forms have always remained at local level, even in the late 1990s when the DfEE gave significant grants to LEAs and careers services to provide programmes of staff development for careers education and guidance. The professional associations, particularly the NACGT (later ACEG) continued to lobby the government to improve professional development for careers education. In 2008 it appeared that these efforts had been rewarded. The DCSF commissioned research into the role of careers co-ordinators in schools and to explore the possibility of a national professional qualification. The research was carried out by the National Foundation for Education Research (NFER), in collaboration with the National Institute for Careers Education and Counselling (NICEC), and published on the same day as the IAG strategy and the statutory guidance on impartial careers education. The research found widespread support for a new, national qualification for careers co-ordinators (McCrone, Marshall, White, Reed, Morris, Andrews and Barnes, 2009) but, by the time the report was published it had become clear that, as a result of the 2008 recession, there would not be the funding available to support the implementation of a national qualification. Therefore access to an appropriate professional qualification for careers co-ordinators remained dependent on what courses were available locally and the extent to which schools would support staff to take the qualification.

School careers co-ordinators in 2010

This chapter is the third section of the history of careers education in schools. In the first chapter mention was made of the first careers teacher, a teacher working in Eastbourne College in 1920. For the next eighty years or so careers teachers continued to be subject teachers who were given additional responsibilities for careers education and guidance, but in the decade covered by this chapter the situation changed. Partly as a consequence of the workforce remodeling reforms in schools, including, in particular, the replacement of management allowances with teaching and learning responsibilities, and partly following a recognition that subject teachers with a substantial teaching timetable often struggled to commit the time needed to ensure good quality careers work, schools began to appoint to the role of careers co-ordinator people from professional backgrounds other than teaching. These 'non-teachers' came from a range of previous job roles – teaching assistants, learning support assistants, school librarians, human resources managers, careers advisers, police officers, armed services, retail managers, banking and financial services, etc.. Careers co-ordinators who were qualified teachers and possibly feared for their jobs, thought schools did this because it was a cheaper option. But the opposite is true. Removing responsibility for careers education and guidance from a member of staff who is a subject teacher saves, in financial terms, only the responsibility allowance allocated to the post and a few hours a week of non-teaching time. Employing a 'non-teacher' on possibly a lower salary but for, say, 25 hours a week costs more money so why did many schools move to this model?

The main reasons given by headteachers were that the careers co-ordinator who is not a teacher has more time to devote to the role, the flexibility to respond to pupils, parents, teaching staff, visiting employers and careers advisers at the most appropriate times and relevant experience and expertise from their previous role (Andrews, 2005). Careers co-ordinators not constrained by a heavy teaching timetable could offer better value for money. Research evidence, suggests, however that there were challenges. Careers co-ordinators who were not teachers required professional development and management support in order to fulfill effectively those parts of their role that were concerned with planning schemes of work for careers education, briefing and supporting teachers of careers lessons and monitoring teaching and learning in careers education. Many 'non-teacher' careers co-ordinators soon became confident IAG managers; it took a bit more time to become comfortable with the subject leadership of careers education in the curriculum.

The NFER/NICEC study quoted in the previous section found that one in four schools had a careers co-ordinator from a background other than teaching. This was based on data collected at the end of 2008. Anecdotal evidence indicated that it became an increasing trend in subsequent years. As careers co-ordinators who were qualified teachers retired, or moved on to other posts, schools replaced them with individuals who were not teachers. The main reason the National Association of Careers and Guidance Teachers (NACGT) changed its name to the Association for Careers Education and Guidance (ACEG) in 2006 was to reflect the fact that a growing proportion of its members were not teachers. A survey published by The Careers & Enterprise Company ten years on from the NFER/NICEC study found that in over 40% schools today the member of staff with lead responsibility for careers is not a qualified teacher (Tanner, Percy and Andrews, 2019). The changes in approaches to leading and managing careers work in schools and the evolution of the role from careers co-ordinator to careers leader are the subject of a new section in chapter 5 of this book.

By the end of the first decade of the 21st century, over forty years after it first appeared on school timetables, careers education had a place in the statutory secondary curriculum, benefited from support at both national and local levels and was being led and managed in schools by careers co-ordinators from a variety of backgrounds, only some of whom had a professional qualification in careers work. This represented significant progress over time and, despite some set-backs along the way, the overall direction had been forward. Nevertheless, careers education was not yet sufficiently well embedded into school practice to become an accepted part of the core curriculum for all pupils. In many schools careers co-ordinators still had to make the case for curriculum time and careers education lessons were often seen as a low priority when it came to decisions about staffing. The support for careers education that had been strengthened over the decade through policy and resources needed to be sustained but, as we will see in the next chapter, progress was dealt a severe blow at the beginning of the second decade of the present century.

References

Andrews, D. (2005). *Careers Co-ordinators and Workforce Remodelling.* Cambridge: NICEC

Central Office of Information (2009). *Unleashing Aspiration: The Final Report of the Panel on Fair Access to the Professions.* Online http://www.bis.gov.uk/assets/biscore/corporate/migratedd/ publications/p/panel-fair-access-to-professions-final-report-21july09.pdf (accessed 26 January 2011)

Connexions Service National Unit (2001). *Connexions for all.* Sheffield DfEE

Department for Children, Schools and Families (2007). *Quality Standards for Young People's Information, Advice and Guidance* (IAG). Sheffield: DCSF

Department for Children, Schools and Families (2008). *Delivering 14-19 Reform: Next Steps.* London: DCSF

Department for Children, Schools and Families (2009a). *Quality, Choice and Aspiration.* London: DCSF

Department for Children, Schools and Families (2009b). *Statutory Guidance: Impartial Careers Education.* London: DCSF

Department for Children, Schools and Families (2010). *Resources Pack to help schools/PRUs implement the Statutory Guidance: Impartial Careers Education.* Sheffield: DCSF

Department for Education and Employment (2000a). *Careers Education in the New Curriculum.* Sheffield: DfEE

Department for Education and Employment (2000b). *Preparing pupils for a successful future in learning and work.* Sheffield: DfEE

Department for Education and Employment (2000c). *School Improvement: How careers work can help.* Sheffield: DfEE

Department for Education and Employment (2000d). *Connexions: The best start in life for every young person.* London: DfEE

Department for Education and Employment (2000e). *Establishing the Connexions service in schools.* Sheffield: DfEE

Department for Education and Employment (2001). *First Impressions: Career-related learning in primary schools.* Sheffield: DfEE

Department for Education and Skills (2003a). *Careers Education and Guidance in England: A National Framework 11-19.* London: DfES

Department for Education and Skills (2003b). *14-19: opportunity and excellence.* London: DfES

Department for Education and Skills (2003c). *Every Child Matters.* London: DfES

Department for Education and Skills (2004). *14-19 Curriculum and Qualification Reform: Final Report of the Working Group on 14-19 Reform.* London: DfES

Department for Education and Skills (2005). *Report of the End-to-End Review of Careers Education and Guidance.* London: DfES

Department for Education and Skills (2006). *Youth Matters: Next Steps.* London: DfES

Edwards, A., Barnes A., Killeen, J. and Watts, A. G. (1999). *The Real Game: Evaluation and the UK National Pilot.* NICEC Project Report. Cambridge: CRAC

Her Majesty's Stationery Office (2005). *Youth Matters.* London: HMSO

Hooley, T., Matheson, J. and Watts, A.G. (2014). *Advancing Ambitions: The role of career guidance in supporting social mobility.* London: The Sutton Trust

Killeen, J., Simmons, P. and Watts, A. G. (1999). *The Effects of Careers Education and Guidance on Attainment and Associated Behaviour.* Cambridge: NICEC

Law, B (1996.) A career-learning theory. In Watts, A. G., Law, B., Killeen, J., Kidd, J. M. and Hawthorn, R. (eds) *Rethinking Careers Education and Guidance, 46-71.* London: Routledge

McCrone, T., Marshall, H., White, K., Reed, F., Morris, M., Andrews, D. and Barnes, A. (2009.) *Careers Co-ordinators in Schools.* London: DCSF

McGowan, A., Watts, A.G., and Andrews, D. (2009). *Local Variations: A Follow-Up Study of New Arrangements for Connexions/Careers/IAG Services for Young People in England.* Reading: CfBT Education Trust

National Audit Office (2004). *Connexions Service: Advice and guidance for all young people.* London: NAO

National College for Leadership of Schools and Children's Services (2009). *Impartial careers education: Principles into practice.* Nottingham: National College

Office for Standards in Education (1998). *National Survey of Careers Education and Guidance (Secondary Schools).* London: Ofsted

Office for Standards in Education (2001). *Inspecting Careers Education and Guidance: pre- & post-16 with guidance on self evaluation.* London: Ofsted

Qualifications and Curriculum Authority (1999). *Learning outcomes from careers education and guidance.* London: QCA

Qualifications and Curriculum Authority (2004). *Work-related learning for all at key stage 4.* London: QCA

Qualifications and Curriculum Authority (2007a). *The new secondary curriculum. What has changed and why?* London: QCA

Qualifications and Curriculum Authority (2007b). *PSHE: Economic wellbeing and financial capability. Programme of study (non-statutory) for key stage 3.* London: QCA

Qualifications and Curriculum Authority (2007c). *PSHE: Economic wellbeing and financial capability. Programme of study (non-statutory) for key stage 4.* London: QCA

Qualifications and Curriculum Authority (2008). *Career, work-related learning and enterprise 11-19. A framework to support economic wellbeing.* London: QCA

Tanner, E., Percy, C. and Andrews, D. (2019). *Careers Leaders in Secondary Schools: The first year.* London: The Careers & Enterprise Company

73

Chapter 4

Careers education in the 21st Century: the second decade

The first three chapters have chronicled the development of careers education in schools in England, from its beginnings midway through the last century to the end of the first decade of the present century. They tell a story of advances and setbacks, of periods of optimism and adversity, but by the beginning of 2010 the position of careers education in schools in England was as healthy as it had ever been, although perhaps not as good as it needed to be. This fourth chapter sets out what happened in the next ten years; a period which started with the first major reversal in securing careers education in the curriculum and then featured a series of developments that sought to preserve its place in schools. As we shall see by the end of the chapter, despite the increased attention on improving career guidance in schools, more work is still needed to ensure that all young people have access to a good quality programme of careers education that helps them to gain the knowledge, understanding and skills needed to take control of their futures.

Early 2010

The decade started well. At the beginning of 2010 the Department for Children, Schools and Families (DCSF) published a substantial pack of resources (DCSF, 2010) to support schools with the implementation in practice of the government's statutory guidance on careers education issued the previous year (DCSF, 2009a). This completed the set of three publications to support careers education in schools: the IAG strategy (DCSF, 2009b); the statutory guidance on impartial careers education; and the resources pack. The materials proved to be extremely popular and within a few weeks the entire print-run of 10,000 copies had been distributed. Fortunately all the components of the pack could also be downloaded from the Careers Education and IAG Support Programme's website (www.cegnet.co.uk). In fact curriculum leaders for careers education in schools often found it more effective to use electronic copies of many of the materials, particularly the audit and diagnostic tools.

By 2010 careers education had been a statutory part of the school curriculum in England for 12 years and for the latter six years this applied throughout key stages 3 and 4, i.e. for all pupils aged 11 to 16. Further, the IAG strategy stated the government's commitment to introducing a pupil guarantee that would include an entitlement to high quality programmes of careers education;

its support for pilots of careers-related learning in key stage 2, with a view to informing the introduction of economic wellbeing into the new primary curriculum proposed for 2011; and its ambition to extend the statutory duty on schools and colleges to provide careers education to pupils and students up to age 18. This last point was linked to a new requirement for young people to remain in education or training beyond the statutory school leaving age of 16, introduced in the Education and Skills Act 2008. From 2015 all young people have been required to remain in some form of learning to age 18.

At the beginning of 2010, therefore, the statutory basis for careers education was strong and supported by well received national guidance and resource materials. Teachers and others with responsibility for planning and developing programmes of careers education in schools had access to help and support through both the CEIAG Support Programme and the IAG Strand of the 14-19 workforce support programme managed by the Specialist Schools and Academies Trust (SSAT). This national and regional support was complemented, in most parts of the country, by consultancy and in-service training provided at local level by Connexions and in some areas careers co-ordinators also had access to certificate and diploma courses of professional development provided by universities, often in partnership with local Connexions services. Further support was offered through Aimhigher, a government-funded programme managed at a regional level by partnerships of universities, colleges and schools, and which aimed to widen participation in higher education, particularly among young people from backgrounds not traditionally well represented. Support was also made available through a national network of local education-business partnerships (EBPs), which supported schools with organising work experience, enterprise activities and other forms of work-related learning, and which received some of their funding through a government grant. In terms of national policy and support from outside, the position of careers education in schools was very positive.

Two other developments appeared likely to further reinforce the position of careers education. Firstly, the government proposed to bring forward legislation to make personal, social, health and economic (PSHE) education compulsory. Although much of the debate about this proposed change focused on strengthening the place of sex and relationships education in the curriculum, in the 2007-08 secondary curriculum review PSHE education had been redefined to include careers education, work-related learning, enterprise and personal finance education. Careers education was already a statutory part of the curriculum but making PSHE education statutory too could only strengthen the place of its component parts. Secondly, the IAG strategy established a Task Force on the Careers Profession which was due to report in the summer of 2010. The hope at the time was that the task force would include within its remit the question of professional qualifications for careers co-ordinators in schools, as well as for careers advisers, and therefore revive the possibility of a national qualification for careers co-ordinators that seemed to have been lost by the time that the research on this issue, commissioned by the DCSF, was published (McCrone, Marshall, White, Read, Morris, Andrews and Barnes, 2009).

While statutory requirements and ready access to support and training provide conditions for good practice, they do not by themselves guarantee high quality provision. The report of a thematic inspection of information, advice and guidance included the finding that the quality of careers education in schools varied considerably, from good to unsatisfactory (Ofsted, 2010). Despite careers education being a compulsory subject, and schools having access to support and training which was usually free of charge, programmes in schools were of inconsistent quality. Other factors were presenting barriers to the development of good quality programmes of careers education. The survey report suggested that schools were not always selecting the most effective curriculum model or giving due priority to careers education when allocating staff to teach programmes. It quoted as poor practice schools providing careers education through tutorial time and others asking staff to teach careers education simply because they had time available on their timetables. Earlier chapters have referred to the advantages and disadvantages of different ways of organising careers education in the curriculum but the 2010 survey indicated that either schools had not reviewed their models of delivery or they had but other factors meant that they had not changed their practice. Similarly, reference has also been made in previous chapters to staff in schools confusing careers education, careers guidance and careers information, and to senior leaders not always seeing the positive relationship between good careers education and guidance and levels of pupil achievement. In its work on IAG the National College for Leadership of Schools and Children's Services found that while headteachers and other senior leaders could see the value of guidance in helping pupils make choices in 14-19 learning, they did not necessarily regard careers education as being quite so relevant. Sometimes this was based on an outdated view that careers education consisted mainly of lessons about jobs.

In summary, at the beginning of the second decade of the present century, conditions were in place to develop good quality careers education programmes in schools but more needed to be done to ensure this happened in practice. A solid foundation had been established but this was about to be undermined.

The Coalition Government

In April 2010 the Labour government, which had been in power for 13 years, called a general election for the following month. An Education and Skills Bill was still making its way through parliament and in the so-called 'wash-up' period prior to the election ministers negotiated with the opposition parties over which sections of the Bill they would support. As a result both the pupil and parent IAG guarantees were dropped, as too was the proposal to make PSHE education a statutory subject. The Labour Party promised to reinstate these sections if re-elected but the outcome of the election was not a fourth term of office for New Labour. The opportunities to strengthen the position of careers education were lost.

There was no outright winner of the election. After several days of negotiation the Conservative Party and the Liberal Democrats formed a Coalition government and published a Coalition Agreement, setting out the broad components of their proposed programme for a full, five-year term of office. Two of the Coalition's main objectives - reducing the economic deficit and reducing state control - were to have significant implications for careers education and guidance for young people in the years ahead, but before examining those changes, it is worth noting the impact of some of the actions taken in the days immediately after the formation of the Coalition. Almost the day after he was appointed to the post of Secretary of State for Education, Michael Gove changed the name of his department from the DCSF back to the Department for Education (DfE), signalling his intention to re-focus on schools and teaching. The new departmental website carried the message that while the content reflected current legislation it did not necessarily represent the new government's policy, thereby indicating that policy changes were likely in the near future. Only a little while later came announcements about not continuing with the new Diplomas and, instead, establishing a new review of vocational education, plus the decision not to go ahead with the introduction of a new primary curriculum.

An immediate consequence of the decision to drop the Diplomas was the closure of the 14-19 workforce support programme which included the IAG strand managed by the SSAT. Another significant impact was the collapse of the local collaborative arrangements between providers which had been established to support the introduction of the Diplomas. These consortia had provided useful forums for local cooperation between school and colleges and between teachers and careers professionals. The review of vocational education, led by Professor Alison Wolf, resulted in policy changes with regard to work-related learning in schools. The report concluded that blanket work experience for all pupils in key stage 4 had served its time and that the DfE should evaluate models for work experience in post-16 education (Wolf, 2011). Wolf went on to recommend that the government should remove the statutory duty on schools to provide work-related learning at key stage 4. The last of the early announcements, about not introducing a new curriculum in primary schools, was to have implications for the pilots of career-related learning in key stage 2. Although the pilots continued and an evaluation report was published (Wade, Bergeron, White, Teeman, Sims and Mehta, 2011), any plans to promote the findings and implement economic wellbeing in the curriculum for key stages 1 and 2 were dropped. It was to be another seven years before the idea of promoting career-related learning in primary schools was re-visited, as will be described later in this chapter.

As the new government turned its attention to tackling the problems in the economy, a key part of its strategy was to make major reductions in public spending. While the government gave a commitment to protect schools' budgets, other areas of education expenditure were cut, including several that related directly to careers education and careers guidance. After nine years, central government funding for the CEIAG Support Programme was stopped. Still only in May and less than three weeks after the election, the government announced reductions in local authority funding and, in particular, a 24% in-year cut in the Area Based Grant (ABG). One of the services funded through the ABG was Connexions. While some local authorities managed reductions of only 7-10% in the service, others cut their services by half and a few decided to close Connexions down altogether, or certainly the element that provided the universal careers guidance service while retaining that part of the service targeted at young people at risk of becoming not engaged in education, employment or training (NEET). One part of the Connexions service that was hit particularly badly in many areas was the support to schools for careers education, as local authorities strived to maintain the IAG service to individual young people with a much reduced budget. It should be noted also that funding for other sources of support was significantly reduced or removed altogether. The Aimhigher programme was closed in 2011, to be replaced later with the more tightly-focused National Collaborative Outreach Programme with less funding. At the same time the substantial grant that EBPs received to support work experience in schools was also removed. These changes, however, were only precursors to a bigger set-back that was to come and from which we are still recovering.

The biggest change to careers guidance for young people in 40 years

The previous chapter described the recurring and persistent concerns about the priority given to careers guidance within Connexions, and the government's responses to those concerns. The final position of the Labour government had been a promise to review local authorities' delivery of IAG in 2011. The Conservative Party's manifesto for the May 2010 General Election included a commitment to replace Connexions with an all-age careers service, and thereby move to the type of arrangements that had been established in Wales, Scotland and Northern Ireland following devolution in those respective parts of the UK. In the summer of 2010 the Coalition government launched a new adult careers service called Next Steps and in November, speaking at the Institute of Careers Guidance (ICG) annual conference, John Hayes, a minister in both the DfE and the Department for Business, Innovation and Skills (DBIS), announced the government's intention to replace the Connexions and Next Steps services with an all-age careers service. The new service would be jointly funded by the DfE and DBIS. However, by the time the service was launched in April 2012, and by then branded as the National Careers Service, it had become clear that it was funded to provide face-to-face guidance services for adults only. The DfE was only prepared to contribute sufficient funding to provide a web-based and telephone service for young people.

Under Michael Gove, the DfE had other ideas for the careers guidance service for young people. In 2011 the government published an Education Bill which proposed a new duty on schools and colleges to secure access to independent careers guidance for all pupils in Years 9 to 11, and at the same time it announced plans to consult on whether the duty should be extended down to Year 8 and up to age 18. In other words, the Secretary of State would devolve his statutory responsibility for the provision of careers guidance for young people to individual schools and colleges. The legislation passed through parliament and, under the Education Act 2011, with effect from 2012 all state-funded schools and colleges have had a statutory duty to secure access to independent careers guidance for all pupils and students from Year 8 to age 18. This represents the biggest change in careers guidance services for young people for four decades. For almost 40 years there was a national service, locally delivered, available to all young people and all schools, free of charge. From 2012 schools have had to make careers guidance available to young people, either by commissioning the services of a careers adviser, or careers organisation providing guidance services, or through employing their own careers adviser. The Milburn Report referred to in the previous chapter recommended that the then Labour government should remove responsibility for providing careers IAG from Connexions and instead allocate the £200m spent annually by local authorities on this service to schools to buy in careers guidance services. The government of the day rejected this idea. However, two years later the Coalition government adopted this approach but without passing any of the funding to schools.

From the moment the Bill was first published concerns were expressed about the consequences of the change in policy for careers support for young people. In particular, a serious worry that without any allocation of additional funding schools would not purchase careers guidance services at the level they had received previously free of charge from the national service. Research reports and inspection surveys have reinforced these concerns and campaigning, from not only the careers sector but also the two major professional associations for headteachers and the Association of Colleges (AoC), was intense in the period 2011-2014. A report commissioned by the DfE showed that three years after the implementation of the new policy a third of schools were not meeting their statutory duty (Gibson, Oliver and Dennison-Copper, 2015). The government's continued refusal to fund careers guidance for young people has led to a serious decline in the level and quality of careers guidance available, and to depleted numbers of qualified careers advisers as a result of redundancies and experienced practitioners leaving the profession. There are no signs that any of the political parties have plans to rectify this situation. For the purposes of this book I will confine my commentary to implications of the change in policy for the position of careers education but not before stressing that the campaigning and lobbying to restore a national careers guidance service for young people needs to be continued. Someone also needs to document the story of careers services in England from the point at which David Peck's (2004) excellent analysis ends with the setting up of Connexions.

One immediate consequence of the change for careers education was the further loss of consultancy and in-service training support that schools had benefitted from for many years. As reported above, in some areas these teams had already been closed down following the severe reduction in the ABG. Now that local authorities were no longer required, nor funded, to provide a universal careers guidance service, many other areas followed suit.

Removal of the statutory duty to provide careers education

Loss of support for careers education from Connexions, local authorities and other programmes was one factor but the biggest setback came from another aspect of the Education Act 2011. The legislation that gave schools the new statutory duty to secure access to careers guidance also removed from schools the statutory duty to provide careers education. With effect from 2012, schools were no longer required to provide careers education. No satisfactory rationale has ever been given for repealing the statutory duty and it would seem that the reasons are more political and presentational, rather than based on educational arguments. The government had an over-riding concern to reduce what it saw as statutory burdens on schools and so wished to present the new duty to secure careers guidance as replacing an existing duty (to provide careers education) rather than an additional requirement.

At the same time, the government accepted the recommendations of the Wolf Report and removed the statutory duty on schools that had been in place since 2004 to provide work-related learning to all pupils in key stage 4. Michael Gove revealed his true opinion about careers education and guidance when questioned by the Education Select Committee in December 2013. He expressed his view that the government should do more to engage employers with schools and that "we do not need a cadre of careers advisers to operate between the two". There is a wealth of evidence, both from systematic research and from practical experience in schools, that meaningful encounters with employers make a positive contribution to careers education and guidance (see, for example, Buzzeo and Cifci, 2017) but nothing to demonstrate that engaging with employers should replace access to professionally qualified careers advisers. The two are complementary. Indeed, the more inspiration and insight pupils gain from several different employers, the more likely they will need access to impartial careers guidance to help them choose the option that is right for them. Young people need encounters with employers but embedded in a programme of careers education and complemented by access to impartial guidance. In this context it is hard to justify removing the statutory duties to provide careers education and work-related learning and not to provide funding for careers guidance.

However, by 2012 schools were no longer required to provide careers education or work-related learning, the national framework for careers education and guidance and the statutory guidance no longer applied, the national support programme was not being funded and in many areas the local support and training for careers co-ordinators had gone. This was just two years in from the start of a new decade when the position of careers education had been at its height, although not strong enough to withstand the loss of its statutory status and funded support.

The rest of this chapter chronicles the various developments, initiatives and programmes that have been instigated in attempting to restore the position of careers education and possibly strengthen it further.

Frameworks and support: the role of professional associations

One of the first organisations to put in place support for careers education in schools once it had been removed from the statutory curriculum was the Association for Careers Education and Guidance (ACEG), formerly the NACGT. Having lobbied unsuccessfully to have the removal of the statutory duty to provide careers education taken out of the 2011 Education Bill, the professional association for careers teachers and careers co-ordinators in England and Wales, set about writing a recommended framework for careers education in schools in England. Taking account of the fact that the government had removed from schools both the statutory duty to provide careers education in years 7 to 11 and the requirement to provide work-related learning in key stage 4, ACEG took the decision to produce a combined framework for careers and work-related education for schools in England. The Welsh Assembly Government had published a single framework for careers and the world of work a few years previously. ACEG also followed another of the developments in Wales by extending its framework beyond the age of 16. In fact, the association went further by extending the age range covered by the framework to include key stage 2 as well, in an attempt to support the work promoting career-related learning in primary schools that had been dropped by the Coalition government. The new, recommended framework for careers and work-related education in England for 7-19 year-olds (ACEG, 2012) was published in April 2012, to provide continuity of support to schools once the statutory duties were removed from the beginning of the next school year, at which point the frameworks for careers education and for work-related learning, published by the DfE and QCA respectively, ceased to apply.

The ACEG framework combined the widely accepted three aims of careers education (self-development, career exploration and career management) and three elements of work-related learning (learning about work, learning for work and learning through work) into three overarching aims:

- self-development through careers and work-related education;
- finding out about careers and the world of work;
- developing skills for career wellbeing and employability.

17 learning outcomes, covering these three aims, were presented for each of the four phases of education in the 7-19 range (i.e. key stages 2 to 4 and post-16) with progression in learning built into the four sets of outcomes. The framework was well received by careers co-ordinators in schools. The approach was consistent with previous good practice and combining careers education with work-related learning reflected what schools had already started to do in practice. A year later the Association published a practical guide to using the framework. ACEG also helped to make sure that the support that had been provided by the national CEIAG Support Programme continued to be available by contributing financially to the ongoing costs of maintaining and updating the CEGNET website. ACEG had been one of the partners commissioned to run the support programme and, along with the careers company that held the original contract before government funding stopped, VT Careers Management, the Association continued to fund the website. When VT pulled out of the careers sector, the programme received support from another careers company, Adviza. Most of the work on managing the site and keeping it up to date was undertaken by Anthony Barnes, a well-respected careers education consultant and a past president of NACGT.

Not long after the Association had published its framework, and around the time that the practical guide to using the framework was launched, ACEG ceased to exist as a separate professional association for careers teachers and careers co-ordinators. In April 2013 four of the main UK professional associations in the careers sector merged to form a single body for careers professionals, the Career Development Institute (CDI). Two of the main membership bodies, the ICG (for careers advisers) and ACEG (for careers teachers) had been represented on the Task Force for the Careers Profession. The task force was set up by the Labour government in late 2009 and it delivered its report (DfE, 2010) in the summer of 2010 by which time the Coalition government was in power. Encouraged by the chair of the task force, Dame Ruth Silver, the professional bodies had come to work more closely together and formed a Careers Professional Alliance. The associations saw the benefits of working together as they lobbied the new government over its plans for careers guidance services and sought to defend the careers sector from the attacks the profession was under. Four of the six members of the alliance - ACEG, ICG, the National Association for Education Guidance for Adults (NAEGA) and the Association of Careers Professionals International (ACPI) - formally merged into the single, UK-wide professional body, the CDI, from April 2013. Although there were some initial concerns that the voice of the careers teacher might become lost in the larger organisation these have proved to be unfounded. The CDI continues to champion the cause for careers education.

The original ACEG framework has now been revised twice under the auspices of the CDI. The first revision (CDI, 2015) was prompted by the establishing that year of The Careers & Enterprise Company (CEC) and its focus on promoting and supporting schools to work more closely with employers. The work of the CEC will be examined in greater depth later in this chapter but the main feature of the 2015 revision was to place more emphasis on employability and enterprise education, while not losing the framework's focus on the long established aims of careers education. The latest update retains the framework of 17 learning outcomes and demonstrates progression across the four phases of education between the ages of 7 and 19 (CDI, 2018). It is supplemented by a range of useful support materials, including audit, review and planning tools available through the CDI's website. The CDI has recently established an online community of practice for careers leaders in schools, which will provide further support for identifying and sharing appropriate resources for developing and delivering careers education in the curriculum.

Quality awards

In Chapter 2 reference was made to local quality standards and externally-assessed awards as a means of recognising and promoting good practice in careers education and guidance in schools and other education and training providers. Most of these awards were developed in the 1990s and by the middle of the Connexions era there were 25 different awards across England

(Andrews, 2005). At that time the awards were seen as having an important role in helping to make sure schools maintained a focus on careers guidance for all pupils, when the priority of the Connexions service was on the needs of the minority of young people who were facing a wider range of issues that presented barriers to progression in learning and into work. In 2012, when schools were required to secure access to independent careers guidance but not given any additional funding to cover the costs of this new responsibility, there was an ongoing role for the awards in promoting the provision of careers guidance. Schools could only achieve a quality award if they met the new statutory duty to secure access to careers guidance for all pupils. When the statutory duty to provide careers education was removed there was an equally important role for the awards to make sure that schools did not drop careers education from the curriculum. However, by 2012 the number of quality awards had dropped to fewer than 20 as the local Connexions services that managed the schemes experienced significant cuts in their budgets.

Recognising the role that the quality awards could play in helping schools assure pupils and their parents of high quality CEIAG, the Careers Profession Task Force recommended that an over-arching national kitemark should be established to validate the different awards. A conference of quality award managers to disseminate the findings of the 2005 survey had made a similar recommendation. One of the members of the task force, Paul Chubb, who had represented the trade organisation for careers guidance services, Careers England, proposed to convene a meeting to the remaining quality award providers to consider how the report's recommendation could be implemented. With a modest grant from DBIS, and support from Careers England, Paul worked tirelessly with the award providers and the careers professional associations to build a consensus for establishing a national validation scheme which would add value to the local awards and ensure consistency and high standards. This resulted in the founding of the Quality in Careers Consortium, led by a Consortium Board, which established a national validation scheme in 2012. Each of the award providers was invited to submit a proposal to be national validated by the Consortium. The Consortium consisted of the main careers organisations together with professional bodies representing schools, colleges and other learning providers. Over the next few years twelve of the providers achieved national validation for their awards which, for the time being, retained their individual names.

Schools could now have confidence that the quality awards were of equal rigour. All versions of the DfE's statutory guidance on meeting the duty to secure access to careers guidance from 2015 onwards also included a recommendation that schools should work towards a nationally-validated award. However, ministers were hesitant to promote the awards more strongly as they questioned why there was not simply one national award. Again, working with the providers of the different individually-branded awards, the Quality in Careers Consortium managed to secure their agreement to move to a single national award, the *Quality in Careers Standard*, which would be awarded by the providers as licensed awarding bodies with effect from 2017 (Andrews and Chubb, 2017).

One further development took place in 2018. The accreditation criteria for the now single national award were aligned to the Gatsby Benchmarks, which were first put forward in 2014 and which all schools are now expected to use to self-review and plan their careers programmes (Gatsby Charitable Foundation, 2014). The Benchmarks merit a separate section of this chapter but once the quality awards had been brought together into a single national standard, aligned fully to the framework that the government expected schools to follow, the DfE then felt confident in strongly recommending that all schools should work towards the *Quality in Careers Standard* (DfE, 2018). With its additional emphasis on careers education in the curriculum, beyond the expectations of the Gatsby Benchmarks, the Standard serves a vital role in making sure schools provide high quality careers education in the curriculum. The Standard remains voluntary but at the time of writing the DfE has made available to the Quality in Careers Consortium a significant grant to promote the Standard to schools that have yet to commit to working towards it.

The Gatsby Benchmarks

The middle of the second decade of the 21st century saw the publication of a report that has since proved to represent a turning point in the provision of careers education and guidance in English schools. From the moment responsibility for securing access to independent careers guidance was devolved to individual schools, concerns had been expressed about the level and quality of careers guidance available to young people. An early survey by the inspection agency Ofsted (2013) found that only one in five schools were providing pupils with the information, advice and guidance they needed. The report concluded that the new arrangements were not working well enough. Similar concerns were raised by the professional bodies representing both careers organisations and schools. Against this background Gatsby, the charitable foundation of Lord (David) Sainsbury, a former Minister for Science, commissioned Professor Sir John Holman to lead a project to identify good practice in career guidance and to recommend a way to embed such practice in all schools. Back in 2007, in a review of science policies, Lord Sainsbury had noted a growing consensus that the career guidance offered to young people was severely lacking. He and Sir John did not want another report criticising the current system: instead they set out to examine what practical steps could be taken to improve career guidance in England's schools.

John Holman sought support from researchers at the International Centre for Guidance Studies (iCeGS), University of Derby, and consulted on his draft findings with representatives from the careers sector. The team from iCeGS and Gatsby visited six countries where previous studies had judged both career guidance and educational results as good. They also visited a number of independent schools in England considered to demonstrate good practice. The outcome of the study was a framework of eight benchmarks of good practice.

Figure 3. The Gatsby Benchmarks (from Gatsby Charitable Foundation, 2014)

1. A Stable Careers Programme	Every school should have an embedded programme of career education and guidance that is known and understood by pupils, parents, teachers, governors and employers.
2. Learning from Career and Labour Market Information	Every pupil, and their parents, should have access to good quality information about future study options and labour market information.
3. Addressing the Needs of Each Pupil	Opportunities for advice and support should be tailored to the needs of each pupil. A school's careers programme should embed equality and diversity considerations throughout.

4. Linking Curriculum Learning to Careers	All teachers should link curriculum learning with careers.
5. Encounters with Employers and Employees	Every pupil should have multiple opportunities to learn from employers about work, employment and the skills that are valued in the workplace.
6. Experiences of Workplaces	Every pupil should have first-hand experiences of the workplace through work visits, work shadowing and/or work experience, to help their exploration of career opportunities and expand their networks.
7. Encounters with Further and Higher Education	All pupils should understand the full range of learning opportunities that are available to them, both academic and vocational, and in schools, colleges, universities and the workplace.
8. Personal Guidance	Every pupil should have opportunities for guidance interviews with a careers adviser, who could be internal or external, provided that they are trained to an appropriate level. These should be available whenever significant study or career choices are being made, and should be expected for all pupils but timed to meet their individual needs.

The report presented the Benchmarks as an overall framework for a school's careers programme. In a sense Benchmark 1 is the overarching statement and Benchmarks 2 to 8 are the different components of the programme. The vision set out in the report was that all schools should establish a careers programme that included all the activities covered by the eight benchmarks.

In Chapter 1 I made links between the stages of development of careers work in schools identified by Law and Watts (1977) and the Gatsby Benchmarks. There are several similarities between the two frameworks, separated by almost 40 years. The essential elements of a good careers programme remain broadly the same and while the Benchmarks are presented as a coherent set of activities, the report recognises that in implementing them in practice schools will be at different stages of development for each benchmark. As noted back in chapter 1, the Law and Watts framework omitted to emphasise the overall objective of a stable and embedded programme but it is worth noting, in relation to the theme of this book, the greater emphasis the earlier framework places on discrete curriculum time for careers education. Another observation is that the Law and Watts components of a careers programme were presented alongside a framework of aims and objectives for careers education and guidance. The Gatsby Benchmarks constitute only a list of activities, or inputs, and are not linked to any framework of proposed outcomes. This is a point to which I will return in the next chapter: for the time being the Benchmarks are proving to be a very useful tool to help schools determine what to put in place to improve their careers programmes. A discussion of whether they are sufficient and what the overall objectives of the programme should be will need to follow.

Gatsby's commitment to improving careers programmes in schools has continued beyond its influential report. In 2015 the foundation worked with the North East LEP[16] to establish a pilot project to test out how the Benchmarks could be used as a framework to review and develop careers programmes in schools and colleges. The original pilot consisted of 13 secondary schools and three colleges from across the North East region. It was facilitated by an assistant head seconded from one of the participating schools and each school and college was allocated a few thousand pounds of development funding. The interim evaluation shows that the schools and colleges were able to

---

[16] Local Enterprise Partnerships (LEPs) are partnerships between local authorities and businesses, working together on local strategies for economic development. There are 38 LEPs across England.

make significant progress towards meeting most, if not all, benchmarks within two years (Hanson, Vigurs, Moore, Everitt and Clark, 2019). Factors identified as contributing to the successful implementation of the Benchmarks included having a regional facilitator, the sharing of practice between the participating schools and colleges and strong leadership, including careers leaders, in the individual education providers. The interim evaluation also indicates some increase in young people's career readiness and levels of attainment at GCSE, but these findings will be tested further in the final, longer-term evaluation.

The Gatsby Foundation has proved to be a significant player in the politics of careers education and guidance. It has been able to build support for its approach over a number of years to a point where most of the careers sector and the wider education sector have got behind it. There is also emerging signs that other countries are starting to show an interest in the Benchmarks. The success of the pilot and the ongoing work of the foundation with the DfE and The Careers & Enterprise Company have led to the government endorsing the Gatsby Benchmarks and placing them at the heart of its strategy to improve careers programmes in schools and colleges.

The strategy will be examined in the final section of this chapter but before that it is necessary to review two other developments in the middle of the decade. And prior to doing that another feature of the Gatsby report should be noted, namely yet another change in terminology. Careers provision in schools and colleges in England has been bedevilled with seemingly endless changes in language. Early chapters of this book have referred to the use of 'careers education and guidance (CEG)'. More recently the more expansive term 'careers education, information, advice and guidance (CEIAG)' has been used as the overarching label, with careers education, careers information, careers advice and careers guidance as the component elements. The Gatsby report deliberately does not use CEIAG: instead it uses the term 'career guidance' to describe the overall programme and adopts the OECD definition that 'career guidance' includes careers information, careers advice and counselling and careers education (OECD, 2004). While it may be helpful to use the more internationally accepted terminology this presents a potential confusion in England, where the term 'careers guidance' has been used to describe one element of career guidance, namely the one-to-one or small group interventions to help individuals resolve career decisions. Gatsby tackles this potential confusion by using the term 'personal guidance' to describe the one-to-one interventions. However, by dropping the word 'careers' personal guidance could be seen as focussing on a wider range of issues beyond considerations of the individual's future in learning and work. Perhaps it might be better to adopt the term used widely in other countries, 'career counselling'. Returning to the central subject of this book, it seems sensible to adopt the more widely used 'career guidance' instead of the unwieldy five-letter acronym of 'CEIAG' for the overall term but it does run the risk that the place of 'careers education' might get overlooked.

The role of teachers

Gatsby was not the only charitable foundation that took a proactive interest in career guidance in schools in the middle 2010s. Teach First is a charity founded in 2002 to improve education, initially in secondary schools in London and by 2014 it had expanded its work to many other regions of England and into parts of Wales, and into primary schools. The main focus of the organisation's programmes is on teacher development and its work is concentrated on schools serving disadvantaged areas and in challenging circumstances. Teach First recognised the key role that careers and employability education could play in raising levels of attainment and breaking the links between educational outcomes and family income. It commissioned iCeGS at University of Derby to research the role of school teachers in delivering career and employability learning. The study identified six distinct, but related, roles that teachers could play in delivering career and employability learning (Hooley, Watts and Andrews, 2015).

Figure 4. Teachers' roles in career and employability learning (from Hooley, Watts and Andrews, 2015)

Tutorial roles

Career informant	Teachers are trusted adults who have made career decisions and have experiences that could be shared with pupils through informed conversations.
Pastoral support	Tutors have regular and frequent contact with a group of pupils over time and can support them through having conversations about their future plans, referring them to careers advisers and following up career guidance interviews.

Teaching roles

Subject teacher	Subject teachers can help make connections between learning in their subject and careers and the world of work. They can also talk about future progression options from their subject.
Careers teacher	Some teachers may be asked to teach specific career and employability lessons, for example, as part of a discrete careers education programme or as part of the PSHE curriculum.

Leadership roles

Careers leader	A teacher can be appointed to the post of careers leader, careers co-ordinator or head of careers. This is a middle leadership role, responsible for the day-to-day leadership and management of career and employability learning.
Senior leader for careers	A member of the senior leadership team can be given overall responsibility for career and employability learning and be the line manager for the careers leader.

The report went on to identify five levels of continuing professional development (CPD) for these roles. The authors proposed a basic grounding in career and employability learning for all teachers as part of their initial teacher education, to be followed by CPD once in post, again for all teachers, to cover delivering career and employability learning and linking it to subject teaching. They then suggested a programme of CPD for teachers interested in becoming careers leaders and a further programme once careers leaders were in post. Lastly they proposed a programme for senior leaders with overall responsibility for careers and employability learning.

Teach First took the findings from the research at iCeGS and published its proposals for improving career and employability learning in schools (Teach First, 2015). The organisation endorsed the taxonomy of six roles and, as a major provider of teacher training, set out its plans for implementing the recommendations concerning initial teacher education and CPD. Specifically they integrated careers and employability learning into their programme for all trainee teachers, linking this principally to the two tutorial roles. They also established pilot programmes of CPD to cover the two teaching roles and a pilot middle leadership training programme for careers leaders. The first pilot of the Careers and Employability Leaders Programme (CELP) involved 15 teachers who had completed the Teach First two-year training programme and ran from 2015 to 2016. The evaluation of the programme concluded that it was as much a school development programme as a professional development programme (Hooley, Dodd and Shepherd, 2016). A second pilot, with 45 careers leaders, ran from 2017 to 2018. Later the Teach First CELP was to influence the design of the careers leaders training programme that is now a central feature of the government's careers strategy launched in 2017 and implemented from 2018.

The Careers & Enterprise Company

Two years after the policy of devolving responsibility for careers guidance to individual schools and colleges had come into effect, the Secretary of State who had introduced the change, Michael Gove, was moved to another department. Soon after arriving in post his replacement Nicky Morgan announced her intention to improve careers guidance in schools and established The Careers & Enterprise Company. Although the company was set up to support schools with developing their careers programmes, the emphasis of its work in the first three years, from 2015 to 2018, was on increasing the level and quality of employer engagement with schools, taking on some of the types of activity that had previously been provided by the EBPs before they had to become fully self-financed. Whenever the organisation explained its role in that initial phase of its work, it would say that it was focussed on Gatsby Benchmarks 5 and 6. This led to concerns that the emphasis was more on work with employers than on other aspects of careers education and guidance, and that the company would not be doing anything to address the problem of schools not putting in place adequate arrangements for the provision of personal career guidance, or indeed wider careers education.

Working with LEPs the company has successfully established a national network of Enterprise Advisers who are volunteers from business linked to schools, offering advice and support on their careers programmes. The Enterprise Advisers are recruited and supported by Enterprise Co-ordinators who are full-time members of staff employed jointly by the LEPs and The Careers & Enterprise Company. In terms of careers education the increased attention on engagement with employers has helped to improve some elements, particularly helping pupils to learn about the world of work and to develop their employability skills and transition skills such as building networks, making applications and preparing for interviews, but other key elements such as developing an understanding of themselves, the skills of decision-making and planning have not been given the same attention.

Despite continuing to give a high profile to its work on employer engagement the company has not concentrated solely and exclusively on that aspect of careers programmes. In the period between becoming established in 2014 and the launch of the careers strategy in 2017, the company had come to accept the Gatsby Benchmarks as the appropriate framework for its activities and it has gradually extended its work into other aspects of career guidance. The company has, for example, produced an online tool to help schools self-review their progress against all the benchmarks. It has also commissioned a number of research studies to identify best practice and has published several guides to support schools; including one specifically on careers education (Collins and Barnes, 2017). From 2018 it has been given the lead role in implementing the government's strategy for improving careers programmes in schools, as we shall see in the next and final section of this chapter.

The Careers Strategy

Responding to the various reports expressing concerns about the state of careers guidance in schools, the DfE commissioned its own research (op. cit.). The survey, published three years into the implementation of the new policy, (DfE, 2015) found that one in three schools were not meeting their statutory duty to provide independent careers guidance and 16% of schools had dropped careers education from the curriculum. This was the origin of the government's careers strategy which is being implemented as this book is being written. The DfE announced its intention to publish a strategy to improve careers guidance in schools in the summer of 2015 but it took two and a half years to emerge, after several re-drafts. This was mainly due to changes in both Secretary of State and ministers responsible for careers during a period of political turmoil following the referendum on membership of the European Union, held in June 2016. The strategy (DfE, 2017) was eventually launched at the CDI's biennial conference in December 2017.

As indicated earlier in this chapter, at the heart of the strategy are the Gatsby Benchmarks. The DfE has been convinced of the value of the framework and expects all schools and colleges to use the Benchmarks to review and improve their careers provision for all pupils and students. The Careers & Enterprise Company has been given an extended brief to co-ordinate support for schools and colleges across all eight benchmarks. The strategy also recommends that all schools and colleges should work towards the externally-assessed *Quality in Careers Standard*. From September 2018 schools and colleges have been expected to publish details of their careers programmes to young people and their parents, and to appoint a named careers leader. The strategy also includes a commitment from government to fund a national training programme for careers leaders, and to set up a series of careers hubs across the country, each consisting of a group of schools and colleges working collaboratively to develop their careers programmes in a similar way to that which operated successfully in the Gatsby pilot in the North East of England.

The publication has been broadly welcomed by the careers sector. It shifts the emphasis away from solely employer engagement to the wider range of career guidance activities reflected in the Gatsby Benchmarks; schools have been given new requirements and expectations to raise the profile of career guidance; for the first time in history the government is prepared to fund a national training programme for careers leaders; and, support is to be provided through the careers hubs. Through the strategy the government has responded positively to many of the representations from the careers profession and from schools and colleges. Further, another of the positive initiatives that had been stopped by the Coalition government in 2010 has been resurrected in the strategy, as funding has been made available for a number of projects to examine best practice in career-related learning in primary schools.

Nevertheless, there remain three areas in particular that the strategy fails to address. Firstly, although the strategy includes funding to research best practice in personal careers guidance, it does nothing to tackle the concerns about the level and quality of careers advice and guidance provided for young people in many schools, nor indeed for those young people who, for whatever reasons, are not in school. None of the funding that local authorities spent on the universal careers guidance service was devolved to schools when they were given responsibility for providing careers guidance: instead schools had to find the money from existing budgets. With no funding, limited support and weak monitoring and regulation, it is hardly surprising that the level and quality of careers guidance available to young people varies considerably from school to school. This remains a major concern in England.

Secondly, very little money has been made available directly to schools to help them build their capacity to improve their careers programmes. The Gatsby pilot showed how much can be achieved with fairly modest levels of development funding. Through the strategy the sources of money available to individual schools are limited to the bursaries to support careers leaders participating in the training programme and any local initiatives funded by the careers hub, if the school happens to be in a LEP area that bid successfully to operate a hub. The Careers & Enterprise Company offers a series of projects and activities but these are always reliant on using designated external partners.

Thirdly, and most closely related to the subject of this book, when drawing up the strategy the government failed to take the opportunity to reinstate the statutory duty on schools to provide careers education. As noted at the beginning of this chapter, this had been removed, without any clearly stated rationale, in 2012. The DfE's own research shows that one in six of schools have since dropped careers education from the curriculum. The government's aim in publishing the strategy was to improve careers provision in schools, and this could have presented an opportunity to not only reinstate the statutory duty but also extend the requirement to age 18. One possible explanation for not taking this action is simply that there was no parliamentary time to introduce the necessary legislation. In 2016 the people of the UK had voted narrowly in a referendum to leave the European Union and for the next three years this one issue has consumed an inordinate amount of parliamentary time. Whatever the reasons, this was an opportunity missed to secure the position of careers education in the curriculum.

At the beginning of the second decade of the 21st century the position of careers education in schools was weakened by the removal of the statutory duty to provide it in the curriculum. One interpretation is that this was not a deliberate action to undermine careers education but collateral damage when a completely new policy for the provision of careers guidance was introduced. However, given Michael Gove's opinions reported earlier in this chapter, it could be viewed as a more purposive act. Over the years that have followed, schools themselves and a number of different organisations have strived to maintain the position of careers education and to support young people's preparation for future study and work. The professional association for careers leaders, the CDI, has published a recommended framework, with supporting resources, for careers education. The Quality in Careers Consortium has ensured that the criteria for achieving the *Quality in Careers Standard* place a strong emphasis on schools having in place a good quality programme of careers education. One of the eight Gatsby Benchmarks requires schools to link curriculum learning to careers. The Careers & Enterprise Company is supporting schools through the Enterprise Adviser Network, a national programme of careers leader training and the rolling out of careers hubs across the country.

Each of these initiatives is well-intentioned and plays a part in supporting the improvement of careers programmes in schools but they have not yet been brought together into a coherent programme of support. Nor, as I will argue in the next chapter, do they all have an explicit reference to careers education. So far the organisations have been working largely in isolation from one another. The Gatsby foundation continues to work with The Careers & Enterprise Company, jointly publishing guidelines, funding research and offering advice on projects. The CDI meets with both organisations, and the DfE, periodically. The Quality in Careers Consortium includes representatives from the CDI and observers from The Careers & Enterprise Company and the DfE. Teach First is one of the providers of the careers leader training programme administered by The Careers & Enterprise Company. All these organisations have played a role in recent years to enhance careers programmes in schools but there remains an untapped potential for them to achieve more by working together.

At the end of the decade careers education remains non-statutory. A national strategy for improving career guidance in schools is being implemented but it remains to be seen if this will restore the position of careers education in the curriculum and, indeed strengthen it, so that all young people are enabled to develop the knowledge and skills they will need for their futures. This chapter brings up to date the history of careers education in schools in England. In the next part of the book I will, firstly, examine the present state of careers education and, secondly, offer proposals for securing a more stable and embedded position for careers education in the school curriculum.

References

Andrews, D. (2005). *Quality Awards for CEG in England: a survey of current availability and uptake.* Cambridge: NICEC

Andrews, D. and Chubb, P. (2017). *The Quality in Careers Standard and quality awards for CEIAG in England. An updated brief history.* http://www.qualityincareers.org.uk/documents/the-quality-in-careers-standard-and-quality-awards-for-ceiag-in-england-a-brief-updated-history-16.3.17.pdf

Association for Careers Education and Guidance (2012). *The framework for careers and work-related education.*   Banbury: ACEG

Buzzeo, J. and Cifci, M. (2017). *Work experience, job shadowing and work-place visits. What works?* London: The Careers & Enterprise Company

Career Development Institute (2015). *Framework for careers, employability and enterprise education.* Stourbridge: CDI

Career Development Institute (2018). *Framework for careers, employability and enterprise education.* Online: https://www.thecdi.net/write/BP556-CDI-Framework-web.pdf (accessed 19 July 2019)

Collins, J. and Barnes, A. (2011). *Careers in the Curriculum. What Works?* London: The Careers & Enterprise Company

Department for Children, Schools and Families (2009a). *Statutory Guidance: Impartial Careers Education.* London: DCSF

Department for Children, Schools and Families (2009b) *Quality, Choice and Aspiration.* London: DCSF

Department for Children, Schools and Families (2010). *Resources Pack to help Schools/PRUs implement the Statutory Guidance: Impartial Careers Education.* Sheffield: DCSF

Department for Education (2010). *Towards a strong careers profession.* London: DfE

Department for Education (2017). *Careers strategy: making the most of everyone's skills and talents.* Online: https://assets.publishing.service.gov.uk/government/uploads/system/uploads/attachment_data/file/664319/Careers_strategy.pdf (accessed 19 July 2019)

Department for Education (2018). *Careers guidance and access for education and training providers. Statutory guidance for governing bodies, school leaders and school staff.* Online: https://assets.publishing.service.gov.uk/government/uploads/system/uploads/attachment_data/file/748474/181008_schools_statutory_guidance_final.pdf

Gatsby Charitable Foundation (2014). *Good Career Guidance.* London: Gatsby Charitable Foundation

Gibson, S., Oliver, L. and Dennison-Cooper, M. (2015). *Mapping Careers Provision in Schools and Colleges in England.* London: DfE

Hanson, J., Vigurs, K., Moore, N., Everitt, J. and Clark, L. (2019). *Gatsby careers benchmark north east implementation pilot: interim evaluation (2015-2017)* Derby: International Centre for Guidance Studies, University of Derby.

Hooley, T., Dodd, V. and Shepherd, C. (2016). *Developing a New Generation of Careers Leaders: An Evaluation of the Teach First Careers and Employability Initiative.* Derby: International Centre for Guidance Studies, University of Derby

Hooley, T., Watts, A. G. and Andrews, D. (2015). *Teachers and careers: The Role of School Teachers in Delivering Career and Employability Learning.* Derby: International Centre for Guidance Studies, University of Derby

Law, B. and Watts, A. G. (1977). *Schools, Careers and Community.* London: Church Information Office

McCrone, T., Marshall, H., White, K., Reed, F., Morris, M., Andrews, D. and Barnes, A. (2009). *Careers Co-ordinators in Schools.* London: DCSF

Office for Standards in Education (2010). *Moving through the system in information, advice and guidance.* Manchester: Ofsted

Office for Standards in Education (2013). *Going in the right direction? Careers guidance in schools from September 2012.* Manchester: Ofsted

Organisation for Economic Development and Co-operation (2004). *Career Guidance and Public Policy; Bridging the Gap.* Paris: OECD

Peck, D. (2004). *Careers Services. History, policy and practice in the United Kingdom.* London: RoutledgeFalmer

Teach First (2015). *Careers education in the classroom. The role of teachers in making young people work ready.* London: Teach First

Wade, P., Bergeron, C., White, K., Teeman, D., Sims, D. and Mehta, P. (2011). *Key Stage 2 career-related learning pathfinder evaluation.* DfE Research Report DFE-RR116. London: DfE

Part II
The present and the future

Chapter 5

Careers education in England: a review of the current position

Part 1 of this book tells the story of the development of careers education in schools in England, from its origins in the previous century through to the end of the 2010s. Throughout its history there has never been a time when the position of careers education has been totally secure. There was a point around the turn of the century when conditions were at their most favourable. Secondary schools had a statutory duty to provide careers education in the curriculum and the government issued a national framework of recommended learning outcomes and funded a national support programme. In addition, there were two streams of funding to provide further support and training at a local level: the grants for education support and training (GEST) administered by local authorities and in-service training (INSET) budgets managed by the national network of privatised careers services. However, the amount of curriculum time devoted to careers education and the quality of provision continued to vary across schools. Practice was very good in some schools but of a lower standard in too many others. Careers education still had to compete for attention against national curriculum subjects and a relentless focus on examination results. Since that peak period several elements of the supporting infrastructure have been removed or severely eroded. Careers education is no longer a statutory part of the curriculum, the dedicated support programme is no longer funded by government and much of the support at the local level has disappeared. Careers education remains marginalised in many schools and, as the DfE's own research has found, one in six schools have dropped careers education from the curriculum completely (Gibson, Oliver and Dennison-Cooper, 2015).

This chapter analyses the current position of careers education in schools in England, with the aim of understanding what actions might be proposed to establish a firmer place in the curriculum. At the present time there is a particular focus on improving careers provision in schools in England, which has several positive features. We have a government endorsed and funded national strategy which promotes a clear framework of good practice and its implementation is being led by a supportive body, The Careers & Enterprise Company, which is capable of offering strategic leadership and co-ordination. In addition we have a workforce of careers leaders in schools with access to fully-funded, relevant training plus a strong tradition of this work which has generated a lot of resources and experience to draw upon. However, we have yet to harness fully all the contributions from the different partners into a coherent programme of improvement. National organisations such as The Careers & Enterprise Company, Gatsby, the CDI and the Quality in Careers Consortium share a common goal to improve the quality of career guidance for young people but their different work-streams are not at present sufficiently well aligned into an overall strategy for implementation. Plus there are limitations and gaps in the present arrangements: the DfE's strategy is currently only funded for two years; there is very little funding available direct to individual schools; we lack a single, definitive framework of outcomes for career guidance in schools; and, with particular reference to the subject of this book, the place of careers education in the curriculum is not emphasised sufficiently. These points are elaborated in the remainder of this chapter.

The Careers Strategy and the status of careers education

At the end of 2017 the DfE published a strategy for expanding the quality and quantity of careers provision in England (DfE 2017). In 2019 we are half-way through implementing a two-year programme of change and already there is evidence that there is a positive impact on the quality of careers programmes in schools (The Careers & Enterprise Company, 2019). At the heart of the strategy is the framework of Gatsby Benchmarks which is proving to be influential in driving the improvements in schools and colleges. Almost every school has heard of the benchmarks and the surveys show that schools are responding positively and making progress against them. However, neither the careers strategy nor the Gatsby Benchmarks include an explicit requirement or recommendation that schools should provide a programme of careers education in the curriculum.

The strategy refers to research that shows that the provision of careers education in schools is unsatisfactory (Archer and Moote, 2017) but does not make an explicit reference to putting in place a planned programme of careers education in the curriculum. Instead, the DfE sets an expectation that all schools and colleges should use the Gatsby Benchmarks to develop and improve their careers provision. The first and overarching benchmark does state that every school and college should have an embedded programme of career education and guidance but the next seven benchmarks, which set out the elements of a good quality provision of career guidance, do not include a dedicated programme of careers education within the curriculum. Benchmark 4 requires all teachers to link curriculum learning with careers. The value of integrating elements of careers education within subjects has long been acknowledged but the limitations of relying on this approach alone have also been identified. The cross-curricular elements need to be complemented by, and brought together for pupils through, a discrete provision, most commonly delivered as part of a wider programme of PSHE. The main tool that is being used to review schools' progress in making improvements, the Compass tool, poses questions about the provision of careers education delivered through other subjects but limits its inquiry into any discrete provision to asking a simple 'yes or no' question: 'do you provide careers lessons to every year group as part of PSHE?'. The opportunity to review the amount of curriculum time devoted to careers education and the model of delivery in each year group has not been taken. We do not have any clear view on how the provision of careers education in schools has changed since the DfE's research published prior to the careers strategy (op.cit.).

When drafting the strategy the DfE chose not to take the opportunity to reinstate, and possibly also extend, the statutory position of careers education in the curriculum. Legislating to make a subject a statutory requirement does not in itself guarantee good quality teaching and learning: indeed neither does it ensure that all schools will in practice teach the subject. Religious education (RE) has been a compulsory subject for all pupils in all schools since 1944 but not every school teaches RE to all year groups, as numerous Ofsted inspection reports bear witness. We also know that it is possible to have good practice in a subject without it being a statutory requirement. Before 1998 careers education was not a compulsory subject, yet many schools provided planned programmes that were taught well. It has never been a statutory requirement in FE colleges or independent schools yet many such institutions have good programmes of careers education. Nevertheless, removing careers education from the statutory curriculum in 2012, after it had been a compulsory element for two generations of secondary school pupils, gave out a message that it was less important and it is, therefore, little surprise that in 2015 the DfE found that 16% of schools had dropped the subject completely (op. cit.).

If parliamentary time could not be found to legislate for the re-introduction of careers education into the curriculum, it is disappointing that the DfE did not include in the strategy a stronger recommendation for schools to provide programmes of careers education. One way the government could have done this would have been to work with the Gatsby charitable foundation to add an explicit reference in the Benchmarks. Specifically, Benchmark 4 could have been re-drafted to incorporate discrete careers education as well as career learning linked with other subject learning. The Gatsby framework seems to dismiss, or at least ignore, the idea that careers education should exist as a separate subject.

Curriculum models

Schools are free to structure the curriculum in whatever way they choose. The advantages and disadvantages of different approaches to organising careers education have been discussed in previous chapters but it is worth revisiting the main issues in this debate in light of the Gatsby Benchmarks seeming to favour an exclusively cross-curricular approach.

Over the years six different models for organising careers education in the curriculum have emerged at different times. In the early days secondary schools would allocate separate lessons for careers education, particularly in the years that now constitute key stage 4. Pressures on curriculum time, certainly since the introduction of the National Curriculum, have resulted in this model virtually disappearing except in special schools and pupil referral units, where there is less emphasis on examination subjects. More commonly discrete careers education is now delivered in one of three different ways: as a module within a carousel of PSHE topics; as an integrated part of a PSHE course, organised within the main timetable and taught by a specialist team of PSHE teachers; or, as part of a structured tutorial programme. Inspection and research evidence indicates that the second of these three models is the most effective: the carousel of modules approach can lead to some groups of pupils receiving their careers education too early, or too late, in the year; the tutorial approach relies on all tutors being fully committed to teaching the programme and on the tutor time not being taken for other activities (DfE, 2011). The integrated PSHE course works effectively when it is taught by a team of teachers who are confident with the content and teaching approaches and the careers education elements are planned to link with related aspects of PSHE and at the most appropriate time of the year. In more recent times some schools have dispensed with their PSHE programmes in the regular timetable and have instead delivered these elements of the curriculum, including careers topics, through a series of whole days or half days. This approach can be very effective for certain topics, such as mock interviews or enterprise projects, but as a means of enhancing a separately-timetabled element, not replacing it.

The sixth approach is to deliver careers education through other subjects. This model has never been fully explored or tested as a sole means of delivery. When cross-curricular approaches were being promoted in the early days of the National Curriculum they largely failed in practice because not all subject teachers were willing to take on responsibility for teaching elements of careers education in addition to the demands of what were then very detailed and prescriptive programmes of study. Evidence from the North East pilot of the Gatsby Benchmarks and the first year of the careers strategy indicates greater success now, as teachers start to see the benefits of bringing relevance to the subject learning and increasing pupils' engagement in the subject lessons. Nevertheless, linking curriculum learning to careers in all subject areas is a major endeavour. At the moment there are only a few teaching resources to support careers education delivered in subject lessons. Also, as the Teach First report demonstrated, any school seeking to develop its cross-curricular approach to careers education will need to invest in CPD for all is subject teachers (Teach First, 2015).

These models are not mutually exclusive. Experience suggests that relying on one model alone is never sufficient. Ideally schools should adopt a mixed approach, with subject learning linked to careers, a discrete provision to deliver those elements that cannot easily be fitted into a subject scheme of work plus curriculum days to accommodate activities that require a few hours rather than 50-60 minutes to complete. Careers education needs to be part of the curriculum in all years, and not concentrated only around points of transition when choices have to be made, but the balance between different modes of delivery may well change in different key stages. As pupils progress up through the year groups the common core curriculum becomes smaller as more subjects become optional. There will be certain elements of careers education that all pupils will need to experience and so the need of some discrete provision will be become greater further up the age range. It would be helpful if the Gatsby Benchmarks could reflect such good practice.

Linking learning in other curriculum areas to careers is valuable, helping pupils to understand the progression opportunities that follow from the different subjects, in terms of both future study options and possible careers. Furthermore, subject teachers can enhance pupils' learning about careers by illustrating how the knowledge, understanding and skills developed through their subject studies can be applied in the world of work (Andrews and Hooley, 2018). However, even in a school that has a well-developed cross-curricular approach to careers education, where every subject teacher is building into their schemes of work activities to enable pupils to learn about the career opportunities that can follow from their subject and about how the learning in their subject can be applied in the world outside the classroom, there will be some elements of careers education that cannot easily be fitted into subject lessons and for which discrete curriculum time will need to be allocated. These discrete careers education lessons also allow opportunities to bring together the various cross-curricular elements and relate them to the pupils' progress in planning their futures. In the best of practice careers education should be delivered through a combination of discrete lessons and work in all other subjects. By making explicit reference only to the latter approach the Gatsby Benchmarks, which form the central spine of the careers strategy, do not preclude the provision of discrete careers education but neither do they actively encourage schools to complement the cross-curricular provision with separately timetabled lessons.

Curriculum frameworks for careers education

One of the features of good quality curriculum provision is having well-defined aims, objectives and learning outcomes. Where these are made clearly available it becomes much easier to decide upon relevant content and appropriate teaching methods when planning schemes of work and lessons. In the recent past, when careers education was a statutory part of the curriculum, the government published a non-statutory framework of recommended outcomes. The requirement on schools was to provide careers education but decisions about what to teach and how were left to individual schools and careers co-ordinators. The statutory duty helped to make sure all pupils had access to the subject but the non-statutory nature of the framework meant that teachers of careers education could use their professional judgement to design and deliver lessons that responded to the needs, interests and aspirations of their pupils, in their particular localities. Even in the time before careers education was compulsory, schools had access to official, but non-statutory guidelines such as those published by HMI and the various non-governmental curriculum agencies, for example the NCC, SCAA and QCA.

Since the statutory duty was removed there have been no national guidelines for careers education published by the DfE. This represents a gap in the current strategy for improving careers provision: there is no list of intended outcomes for pupils. What is presented instead is a programme of support activities to enable schools and colleges to work on developing their careers programmes, central to which is the framework of Gatsby Benchmarks which specify a number of inputs a school or college should put in place for each and every pupil or student. This is, however, not linked to a statement of what pupils and students should gain and achieve from the programme of activities. Beyond a general aim of wanting every young person to be able to build a rewarding career there is nothing that gives details of the knowledge, understanding and skills that they should be helped to develop through the careers programme. This makes it difficult for schools to be confident that the activities they provide are the most appropriate and to be able to assess whether or not pupils are achieving the desired outcomes.

In the absence of any official guidance there exist several different frameworks that schools are using to assist their planning. The professional body for the careers sector, the Career Development Institute (CDI), has published a framework for careers, employability and enterprise education (CDI, 2018) and while schools are encouraged to use this framework of recommended outcomes it has not been formally adopted or promoted by either the DfE or The Careers & Enterprise Company. Some schools are also using the programmes of study published by the PSHE Association (PSHE, 2017). Ever since the scope of PSHE was extended to include economic wellbeing the recommended programmes of study, particularly those for key stages 3 and 4, have included elements of careers education and many schools deliver careers education lessons through their PSHE schemes of work. In addition several organisations, including the CBI and some of the 38 local enterprise partnerships (LEPs) across England, have published frameworks of employability skills, and these too are being used by some schools to inform their planning of careers programmes. Having recommended objectives and learning outcomes to inform curriculum planning is essential but the multiplicity of frameworks is also potentially confusing. The lack of a single, definitive framework of outcomes that all schools should be encouraged to use alongside the Benchmarks represents another gap in the current strategy.

Quality in Careers Standard

The bringing together of the various different local and regional quality awards in England into a single national standard was described in the previous chapter. The assessment criteria for the *Quality in Careers Standard* have been aligned to the Gatsby Benchmarks and in places they exceed the requirement in the Benchmarks (Quality in Careers Consortium, 2019). One area where this is particularly true relates to the provision of careers education. With reference to Benchmark 4, the criteria for the Standard reiterate the requirement to link curriculum learning to careers but they go on to state that the school or college must provide additional evidence of:

"Embedding careers education in curriculum learning so that every student has the opportunity to benefit from career-related learning and preparation for the future embedded in the curriculum including stand-alone, subject based and planned co-curricular and enrichment activities"
[p.12]

and

"Developing effective approaches to the teaching, learning and assessment of careers, employability and enterprise education that facilitate the career development of students and their transitions…"
[p.13]

These statements provide a lever to encourage schools and colleges to provide good quality careers education. Working towards achieving the Standard is, however, only 'strongly recommended' in the careers strategy and currently only a third of schools in England have either achieved the Standard or committed to working towards it.

The DfE has recently granted funding to the Quality in Careers Consortium to promote the Standard to those schools that have yet to commit. In recent years there has been an ongoing debate about the relationship between the *Quality in Careers Standard* and the Compass tool developed by The Careers & Enterprise Company and Gatsby. The latter is a self-review tool for schools and colleges to use to assess their progress against the Benchmarks, while the Standard is an external assessment of the quality of a school's careers provision. Despite the assessment criteria for the Standard now being fully aligned to the Benchmarks, it is not yet actively promoted by The Careers & Enterprise Company or Gatsby as a means of validating a school's self-assessment. If it were it would provide a way of publicly recognising schools that had achieved all eight benchmarks and offer another incentive for schools to commit to the Standard and thereby work towards developing their careers provision to include, among other elements, a good quality programme of careers education in the curriculum.

Support for careers education

Over the past fifty to sixty years various forms of support and training for careers education in schools have been put in place, as detailed in Part I of this book. This chapter is concerned with a review of the current position. From the point at which the statutory duty to provide careers education was removed the national programme of support became reduced and the local infrastructure of careers education and guidance advisers, development managers and careers associations gradually disappeared, confined to only a few areas where the local authority continued to commit limited resources to supporting schools. It should be noted that at the same time the government was actively encouraging schools to become free-standing academies, independent of the local authorities. This had the effect of making it increasingly difficult to maintain a support structure for schools. Later the schools that had become academies were encouraged to come together to form multi-academy trusts (MATs), some of which have recruited staff to provide support for career guidance across the MAT.

In the period immediately before the launch of the careers strategy support for careers education had, therefore, become fragmented and was provided by a mix of local authorities, MATs, the CDI and private organisations, but at different levels across England. In the meantime, The Careers & Enterprise Company was establishing its national network of enterprise advisers (EAs). The EAs are senior personnel from business who have volunteered to give a day a month of their time to support a local school with developing its careers programme. Initially the focus was on helping the school to enhance its engagement with employers but when the careers strategy was published the EAs started to get involved with other aspects of the careers programme. While many schools find the discussions with their EA helpful (The Careers & Enterprise Company, 2018a), the business volunteers have no specific expertise in careers education. The growing network of EAs has the potential to provide a nationwide support structure but it will need to be more closely linked with other forms of support at the local level to be fully effective, particularly with reference to the development of careers education in the curriculum.

The strategy has begun to introduce a new form of support, the careers hubs. The DfE initially committed funding for 20 careers hubs across the country but such was the level of interest when The Careers & Enterprise Company started to establish the hubs that the government announced an extension to 40 hubs. Each hub consists of 20-40 schools and colleges working collaboratively to develop their careers programmes. The concept is based on the successful Gatsby pilot in the North East. Around a quarter of all the schools in England are part of a careers hub and if the hubs were to be extended to all parts of the country they would provide a fully national network which could harness the sources of support at a local level, not only the EAs but also LEAs, LEPs, MATs, EBPs plus other local careers networks.

Training

Over the years training and professional development for careers teachers has been delivered by a variety of public and private sector organisations, university departments, professional bodies, etc., but there has never been a fully funded, national provision. Immediately prior to the publication of careers strategy teachers and other school staff seeking training in planning and delivering careers education could choose to book places on short, usually one-day, courses or conferences organised by local authorities, careers companies, the CDI or a number of private training providers. Anyone looking for a longer course had only a limited number of options at one of the few university departments that had managed to retain its programme despite reductions in budgets for training. The costs of attendance on all these courses, both long and short, had to be covered by the school.

The one exception to this provision was the Careers and Employability Leader Programme (CELP) established by Teach First. The programme originated from the research Teach First commissioned from the International Centre for Guidance Studies, University of Derby into the role of teachers in careers education (Hooley, Watts and Andrews, 2015) and Teach First's proposals for professional development for the six different roles identified in the research (op. cit.). As outlined in the previous chapter, Teach First ran its first pilot programme for 15 careers leaders over eight days in 2015-16 and a second pilot for 45 careers leaders over 12 days in 2017-18. The costs were covered by charitable donations so there was no charge to the schools. The programme covered the full role of leading and managing a careers programme in a school, and planning and delivering a programme of careers and employability education was a key part of the course.

The careers strategy currently being implemented across the country includes, for the first time in England, a fully-funded national programme of training for careers leaders in schools and colleges. This builds on the Teach First pilots and previous courses provided by universities and other training organisations. The DfE initially committed funding to provide 500 places on the careers leader training and gave The Careers & Enterprise Company responsibility for setting up and managing the programme. In 2018 14 providers, including a mix of universities, careers sector training organisations and providers of school leadership training, were commissioned to develop courses comprising four to six days of face-to-face delivery, with online support available between the attendance sessions. At the same time The Careers & Enterprise Company established an online registration process. The level of interest from careers leaders far exceeded the 500 available places and so the DfE increased the funding to cover a total of 1,300 places. Some of the courses lead to an award, while others are unaccredited, giving careers leaders a choice of approach. The places are fully funded by central government and the school also receives a bursary to meet costs such as travel and supply cover.

This development has been warmly welcomed by the careers sector as it provides a major form of support for developing careers programmes in schools. It does, however, represent only one part of the CPD provision that is required. Training also needs to be provided for teachers delivering careers education, either in subjects or as part of a discrete provision. It is very uncommon for careers education to receive any attention during initial teacher education, so some form of in-service training is essential to support the delivery of careers education in schools. This, in turn, will require the training programme for careers leaders to include sessions not only on planning schemes of work for careers education but also on leading CPD for subject teachers and careers teachers.

Careers leaders

In an earlier chapter the changing labels for careers provision in schools were examined. In England, for the time being at least, we appear to have settled on 'career guidance' as the over-arching term for the whole provision and use the terms 'careers information', 'careers education' and 'personal guidance' for the individual elements (although I suspect there will be a lot of discussion about the last item, as advocates of 'careers counselling' and 'career coaching' enter the debate). But it is not only the terms for the programme and its component parts that have changed: the job title of the person leading and managing the programme has similarly changed over time. Early 20th century titles such as 'careers master' and 'careers mistress' soon became replaced by the gender-neutral titles of 'careers teacher' and 'head of careers'. Later, recognising that the job involved bringing together contributions from various other teachers and tutors and that it could no longer be assumed that the person with responsibility for careers in the school was a teacher, 'careers co-ordinator' became the preferred title. In recent years this has been replaced by 'careers leader'.

The title careers leader raises the status of the role and acknowledges that the job involves more than simply co-ordinating a set of activities: it requires the postholder to develop a vision for careers in the school and to lead the implementation of a careers strategy to meet the Gatsby Benchmarks. From the time when the Coalition government passed responsibility for careers guidance to individual schools and colleges in 2012, it soon became clear that there would need to be in each school and college someone who could lead the careers programme and orchestrate all the component parts into a coherent provision for young people. The Gatsby pilot in the North East provided further evidence of the crucial importance of this role. It is for these reasons that another central feature of the current careers strategy is that all schools and colleges must appoint a named careers leader.

Another reason for adopting the term careers leader is that it fits with the language of schools. Schools no longer have senior management teams, they have senior leadership teams. Senior leaders are supported by middle leaders, who include subject leaders and pastoral leaders. It is entirely consistent with these developments that the person leading and managing the careers programme should be called the careers leader.

It is difficult to determine the precise date when the term careers leader was first used. In 2004 the National Institute for Careers Education and Counselling (NICEC) published a briefing on leading and managing careers work in schools (NICEC, 2004). The sub-title was 'the changing role of the careers co-ordinator' but the paper concluded that 'careers work leader' might be a more appropriate description of the role. The paper had its origins in a research project on the career experiences and career development of careers co-ordinators in schools (Andrews and Barnes, 2003) and attempted to identify the different tasks involved in leading and managing the careers provision in a school. It suggested that careers co-ordinators were: *organisers* of activities; *co-ordinators* of programmes; *networkers* within the school and with the wider community; and, *leaders and managers* of an area of the school's work. These labels for aspects of the role can be recognised in the headings of The Careers & Enterprise

Company's guide on the role of careers leader in schools (The Careers & Enterprise Company, 2018b).

Slowly over the past 15 years the term careers leader has become established as the most appropriate title for the role. When the then DCSF commissioned a feasibility study for establishing a professional qualification for careers co-ordinators the unpublished framework for the proposed award was titled 'Qualification in Careers Leadership (QCL)'. Once the term had become officially recognised by government in the careers strategy, The Careers & Enterprise Company was tasked with specifying the role so that schools could make informed decisions about appointing suitable candidates to the position and providers of the careers leader training could design relevant courses. Case studies of effective careers leadership in schools were researched and the findings (Andrews and Hooley, 2016 & 2019) were used to produce the guide on understanding the role. The key responsibilities of the role are listed under the four headings: *leadership; management; co-ordination; networking*. It is recommended that the role should be at middle leader or senior leader level and supported by a careers administrator.

In the first chapter of this book I referred to a list of essential duties for the careers teacher written by a group of headteachers in 1973. There were just seven items, compared with the 30 in the current guide. Each of the seven items can be easily linked to one or more of the present day Gatsby Benchmarks but the last item is more specific about the provision of careers education:

"to plan the use of timetabled time designated for careers work".

The nearest equivalent item is the present day guide on the role of careers leader is:

"planning the programme of activity in career guidance."

The latter is a broader task but less specific about timetabled time. The job has clearly grown in the intervening years but we should be careful not to lose a key feature.

The role of careers co-ordinator should have always combined the roles of 'IAG manager', i.e. managing the provision of careers information and access to careers advice and guidance, and 'subject leader for careers education', i.e. planning the schemes of work for careers education, supporting teachers delivering the careers lessons and monitoring teaching and learning in careers education. In the current context it is for schools to decide whether responsibility for careers education should be retained as part of the careers leader's role or delegated to a colleague within a careers leadership team but responsibility for this area of the curriculum should be clearly assigned to someone. At present this aspect of the role of careers leader is not sufficiently explicit.

Scope of careers education

For over 40 years there has remained a broad consensus about the overall scope of careers education which has its origins in the DOTS framework first proposed by Law and Watts (1977). That is to say that the focus has been on the four aims of helping pupils to understand themselves, to learn about the opportunities available, to know how to make decisions and to develop the skills to manage transitions to the next stage of education, training or employment. The aims have been reframed from time to time, for example into the three aims of self development, career exploration and career management, but the overall purpose has remained the same. In the early days there was a brief period when a debate took place about whether this framework for equipping young people with the skills to find and secure jobs that matched their interests and aspirations should be replaced by something more radical that would aim to equip young people to become empowered as agents of social change, but the status quo prevailed and has persisted right up to the present day. In the next chapter I will put forward a case for reviewing the scope of careers education but in taking stock of the present position I will use the current aims to frame my observations.

In the best of practice schools still have programmes of careers education that pay due attention to all four, or three, aims but there is a suggestion that in recent years there has been a greater focus on helping pupils understand the opportunities available to them and, to a lesser extent, on developing transition skills such as making applications, writing CVs and preparing for interviews, with less emphasis on developing an understanding of themselves and on learning strategies for making career decisions and plans. From the moment The Careers & Enterprise Company was established in the middle of the past decade a lot of resources have gone into increasing schools' work with employers and Gatsby Benchmark 5 requires all pupils to have at least one meaningful encounter with an employer each year. These activities have enhanced work on helping pupils become better informed about opportunities in the world of work and to develop career management and employability skills. There has, however, been less attention on self development.

The absence of a clear framework of aims, objectives and learning outcomes, linked to the Gatsby Benchmarks, is a significant gap in the current strategy. The Benchmarks provide an operational specification of activities but avoid specifying the outcomes that the careers programme should aim to achieve for young people. Schools are using the Benchmarks to put in place improvements to their careers provision but we need to build a national consensus around a framework of learning outcomes to ensure that the activities being put in place lead to pupils gaining the right knowledge, skills and qualities.

In summary

At the time of writing this second edition the DfE in England is implementing a national strategy for improving careers provision in schools. The evidence suggests the actions being taken and the support being put in place are having a positive impact in many schools although there is still a long way to go. The Careers & Enterprise Company's State of the Nation 2019 report identifies only 99 schools and colleges (2% of the total number in England) that have fully achieved all eight benchmarks (op. cit.).

The concern for careers education is that references to this aspect of career guidance are either missing or not sufficiently explicit. It is left to individual schools to determine how much emphasis to place on this important part of the curriculum that should equip young people to progress successfully through learning and into work, with the result that practice varies from very good to poor or inadequate. Opportunities to promote good practice are missed and developments that could help to make a difference are not being brought into a coherent programme of implementation.

The careers strategy presents a major opportunity to secure a stronger position for careers education in schools but the curriculum dimension is currently not sufficiently well emphasised and the support that could be harnessed is still fragmented. The government has only committed funding to support the strategy for two years. This will not be long enough to bring about the sustainable developments that are needed but it does present the opportunity to demonstrate what can be achieved and to make the case for continuing the funding beyond 2020. It will be important to use this time to rectify the gaps in the strategy identified in this chapter.

In conclusion:

- the amount of time devoted to careers education programmes and the quality of provision remains too varied. Examples of good practice exist but it will take some time to bring all schools up to the standard of the best

- careers education has returned to being a non-statutory part of the school curriculum

- the Gatsby Benchmarks place an emphasis on delivering careers education through subject lessons and omit any reference to having in place a discrete programme to complement the cross-curricular provision

- there is no official framework of desired learning outcomes for the careers programmes that schools are expected to put in place, and the framework that has been developed by the professional body is not promoted as part of the careers strategy

- the *Quality in Careers Standard* promotes the need for good quality careers education but schools are only strongly recommended to work towards achieving this national award. The Standard is not being positively promoted as an external validation of schools' self-assessment of having achieved the Gatsby Benchmarks.

- the careers hubs present a significant opportunity to establish a national network of support for schools to develop their provision of careers education within their overall careers programmes, but at present they only cover 25% of the schools in England

- the role of careers leader has been officially recognised and all schools are required to appoint someone to the position. However, the guide to understanding the role does not include the tasks of leading careers education in the curriculum in the list of responsibilities of the role

- the national programme of careers leader training provides an opportunity to ensure that all careers leaders have access to professional development that supports them to develop effective careers programmes that include careers education. The current programme represents initial training for the role of careers leader but at present it is not complemented by a programme of ongoing CPD equivalent to the government-funded GEST and INSET programmes that existed previously or by any incentives for schools to provide CPD for other teachers involved in delivering the careers programme.

The current momentum behind the implementing of the careers strategy into practice in schools offers an ideal opportunity to improve all aspects of career guidance programmes for young people. At present there is a risk that careers education will be overlooked. Actions for improving the provision of careers education in schools in England, based on an analysis of the points summarised above, will be presented in the next and final chapter.

References

Andrews, D. and Barnes, A. (2003). 'Career Development of Careers Co-ordinators'. *Career Research & Development: the NICEC journal*, No. 9 Summer 2003

Andrews, D. and Hooley, T. (2016). '… and now it's over to you: recognising and supporting the role of careers leaders in schools in England. *British Journal of Guidance & Counselling*. DOI: 10.1080/03069885. 2016.1254726

Andrews, D. and Hooley, T. (2018). *The Careers Leader Handbook*. Bath: Trotman

Andrews, D. and Hooley, T. (2019). Careers leadership in practice: a study of 27 careers leaders in English secondary schools. *British Journal of Guidance & Counselling*. DOI: 10.1080/03069885. 2019.1600190

Archer, L. and Moote, J. (2016). *ASPIRES 2 Project Spotlight. Year 11 Students' Views of Careers Education and Work Experience*. London: King's College, London

Career Development Institute (2018). *Framework for careers, employability and enterprise education*. Online: https://www.thecdi.net/write/BP556-CDI-Framework-web.pdf (accessed 19 July 2019)

Department for Education (2011). *Personal, Social, Health and Economic (PSHE) Education: A Mapping Study of the Prevalent Models of Delivery and their Effectiveness, Research Report DFE-RR080*. London: DfE

Department for Education (2017). *Careers strategy: making the most of everyone's skills and talents*. Online: https://assets.publishing.service.gov.uk/government/uploads/system/uploads/attachment_data/file/664319/Careers_strategy.pdf (accessed 19 July 2019)

Gibson, S., Oliver, L. and Dennison-Cooper, M. (2015). *Mapping Careers Provision in Schools and Colleges in England*. London: DfE

Hooley, T., Watts, A. G. and Andrews, D. (2015). *Teachers and careers: The Role of School Teachers in Delivering Career and Employability Learning*. Derby: International Centre for Guidance Studies, University of Derby

Law, B. and Watts, A. G. (1977). *Schools, Careers and Community.* London: Church Information Office

National Institute for Careers Education and Counselling (2004). *Leading and Managing Careers Work in Schools: the changing role of the careers co-ordinator.* NICEC Briefing. Cambridge: CRAC/NICEC

PSHE Association (2017). *PSHE Education Programme of Study key stages 1-5.* Online: https://www.pshe-association.org.uk/system/files/PSHE%20Education%20Programme%20of%20Study%20%28Key%20stage%201-5%29%20Jan%202017_2.pdf (accessed 13 August 2019)

Quality in Careers Consortium (2019). *The Revised Guide to the Standard.* Online: www.qualityincareers.org.uk/documents/jun19-the-guide-to-the-standard.pdf (accessed 13 August 2019)

Tanner, E., Percy, C. and Andrews, D. (2019). *Careers Leaders in Secondary Schools: The first year.* London: The Careers & Enterprise Company

Teach First (2015). *Careers education in the classroom. The role of teachers in making young people work ready.* London: Teach First

The Careers & Enterprise Company and Gatsby Charitable Foundation (2018a). *Evaluation of the Enterprise Adviser Network: School and College Survey 2018.* London: The Careers & Enterprise Company

The Careers & Enterprise Company and Gatsby Charitable Foundation (2018b). *Understanding the role of the Careers Leader. A guide for secondary schools.* London: The Careers & Enterprise Company

The Careers & Enterprise Company (2019). *State of the Nation 2019: Careers and enterprise provision in England's secondary schools and colleges.* London: The Careers & Enterprise Company

Chapter 6

Careers education in English schools: where do we go from here?

Chapter 5 examined the current position of careers education in schools in England. It is almost sixty years since it first started to feature in the curriculum and throughout that period the amount of time allocated to the subject and the quality of teaching and learning have remained inconsistent. Ofsted inspections and surveys have identified examples of outstanding practice but in too many schools the provision of careers education is unsatisfactory and in some it has been dropped from pupils' timetables entirely. We are not helping all of our young people develop the knowledge and skills they need to plan and manage a successful progression through learning and into work.

The government has acknowledged that the provision of careers support in schools and colleges needs to be improved and in 2017 the Department for Education (DfE) published a detailed careers strategy to address the concerns (DfE, 2017. The implementation of this strategy is beginning to have a positive impact on careers programmes (The Careers & Enterprise Company, 2019), although there is still a long way to go until all schools meet the standards that have been adopted to form the central spine of the strategy, the Gatsby Benchmarks (Gatsby Charitable Foundation, 2014). However, the careers strategy omits one component of a complete careers programme, the provision of a discrete element of careers education. In this chapter I present proposals for rectifying this omission and ensuring that the current drive to improve careers programmes in schools (which has been described as 'the Gatsby revolution') includes actions to drive up the quality of careers education in the curriculum, alongside all the other components, so that we can be confident that each and every pupil is fully equipped and enabled to have a rewarding career.

These proposals concentrate on actions for immediate implementation but I also go on to present an argument for a more fundamental, longer-term reform of the school curriculum that places careers education at its heart rather than the peripheral position it has occupied for too long.

Building careers education into the Careers Strategy

The careers strategy is being implemented as this second edition is being written. It will take longer than the current two-year period of funding to achieve the improvements required and it is hoped that the government will, therefore, continue to fund the programme beyond 2020. This would provide the opportunity to incorporate additional actions into the strategy with the aim of improving the quantity and quality of careers education in schools. The review of the current position presented in the previous chapter identified that careers education has been overlooked in the strategy and the proposals that follow are put forward as an additional strand of the careers strategy to enhance the provision of careers education for young people.

Careers education in the curriculum as a component of career guidance

It is worth reminding ourselves of the place of careers education in the overall provision of careers support. Prior to recently adopting 'career guidance' as the overarching term to describe the complete provision, the DfE and others in England used the slightly unwieldy, five-letter acronym, CEIAG. Although this terminology had to be interpreted when making international comparisons it did have the advantage of reminding policy-makers and practitioners that careers programmes have three constituent elements: careers education; careers information; careers advice and guidance. As the history of the development of careers education in England schools described in Part I of this book has shown, careers education was the most recent addition to the programme. Early forms of careers support for young people consisted solely of providing information on different opportunities in further study and work, and access to advice and guidance to help pupils make appropriate choices. It was only later that the value of enabling pupils to assess their strengths and interests, research options, and develop the skills to make choices and manage transitions, was recognised. When careers education was first introduced into the curriculum it was usually viewed as having a supportive role in relation to careers guidance, i.e. to prepare young people for the careers interview at which key decisions would be made (Morris, Simkin and Stoney, 1995). Today it is recognised that decisions about what courses and subjects to study at school, and about what route to take on leaving school, are only the first of several career decisions that will need to be made throughout life. Alongside access to careers information, advice and guidance, individuals also need a set of career management skills for life, plus knowledge and understanding of the nature of career in the 21st century.

Careers today are very different from those at the time when careers guidance services were first established for young people.

Pupils leaving school now are likely to have ten or more different jobs in their working life and probably at least one change of occupation. To progress successfully through such careers they will need lifelong access to up to date and accurate information about the opportunities available, timely advice and guidance and a set of skills for planning and managing their career moves. This is a point that was stressed as recently as 2016 in a research paper published by The Careers & Enterprise Company (2016), after the publication of the Gatsby report but before the launch of the careers strategy.

"Reducing the 'cognitive burden' of choices …requires better information, better career guidance support, and an education that builds [young people's] confidence and capabilities with regard to decision making."
[p.4]

The last part of that quotation is an accurate definition of careers education.

The case for allocating time in the curriculum to equip pupils to make choices in learning and the labour market seems obvious, so questions remain about why schools do not always do this in practice and about why the careers strategy does not include an explicit reference to making time available for careers education. The answers to the first question lie in how the performance of schools in England is measured and the demands of the National Curriculum. While secondary schools continue to be judged on pupils' examination grades, and remain required to teach a prescribed content for a list of traditional subjects, there will be less attention paid to careers education, despite headteachers and governors acknowledging its value.

The second question is more difficult to answer. The careers strategy adopts the framework of the Gatsby Benchmarks, which themselves are based on observations of good practice. It is possible that the research team did not see examples of good careers education in the six countries they visited. It does not necessarily follow that it should, therefore, not be included in the curriculum. Perhaps those countries are also struggling to secure good quality careers education for all pupils. We know from other international studies that in several countries that are deemed to have developed a good provision of career guidance, careers education is included as a subject in the school curriculum (for example, in Denmark and Norway). In the past other countries have taken some of the ideas generated in England to inform developments in careers education in their own schools. One only has to study the various frameworks for careers education used across the world to see the influence of the Law and Watts DOTS framework for example. There is a growing interest internationally in the Gatsby Benchmarks and how they are being implemented in England. If we could incorporate careers education into the strategy the lessons learned might benefit not only pupils in schools in England but young people in other nations as well.

Bringing the scope of careers education up to date

If we are on the threshold of making a difference to the provision of careers education in schools, it would be worth not only restating the value of careers education alongside careers information and careers advice and guidance, but also reappraising its aims in relation to how careers are now lived. Traditionally programmes of careers education have concentrated on the knowledge and skills needed to plan and manage successful progression and transitions through learning and into work. But such work on career management skills needs to be enhanced if schools are to fully prepare pupils for careers in the 21st century. We are living in a digital age and most young people will be researching careers information via the internet, networking with others through social media and making applications online. This calls for a set of digital career management skills. Hooley (2012) has identified seven such competencies which do not replace existing frameworks but need to be incorporated into the established aims of careers education.

Figure 5. The seven 'Cs' of digital career literacy (from Hooley, 2012)

Digital career management skill	Definition	Broad careers education aim to which the competency relates
Changing	the ability to understand and adapt to changing career contexts	Career exploration
Collecting	the ability to find, manage and retrieve career information	Career exploration

Critiquing	the ability to evaluate, analyse the provenance of and assess the usefulness of career information	Career exploration
Connecting	the ability to make contacts, build relationships and establish networks online that support career development	Career management
Communicating	the ability to interact effectively across a range of different platforms and to understand the 'netiquette' of different interactions and to use them in the context of career	Career management
Creating	the ability to create online content that represents their interests, skills and career history	Career management
Curating	the ability to develop, review and edit their online presence	Self development

There is one further set of skills that careers education needs to encompass. Traditional frameworks have always extended beyond the skills required to find and secure opportunities in learning and work, to include the skills and qualities required not only to cope and survive in the next phase of study or employment but also to succeed and thrive. The 'T' in DOTS refers to transition learning, and this aspect of careers education is not limited to the skills needed to find and secure jobs or places on courses. It also covers the skills and qualities needed to settle into the job or onto the course and to do well. Transition learning, therefore, should not only teach application skills, such as writing a targeted CV and preparing presentations, but also help pupils understand what the next stage will be like and the skills they will need to succeed in that environment. In more recent times this latter aspect has received a lot of attention in respect to young people preparing for the workplace. Various different organisations have identified lists of what have become known as employability skills, the generic skills required to succeed in the workplace in any job. The lists typically include such skills and qualities as communication, teamwork, problem-solving, interpersonal, organisational, initiative, reliability, flexibility and honesty. There is no single definitive list but there is a consensus that such skills and qualities should be part of a careers education programme. Not all of the encounters that schools arrange with employers are talks about particular jobs or businesses, many of them focus more on helping pupils understand the need for these employability skills.

All individuals will need employability skills if they are to succeed in work but there is another set of skills that pupils will need more immediately on leaving school. Reference has been made already in this chapter to the changing nature of careers. One way in which careers are changing is that in England we have delayed young people's entry into the labour market. In the 1960s, when careers education first appeared on school timetables, the school leaving age was 15. By the time the DOTS framework was published it had been raised to 16, but still the majority of pupils left school at this age and went into jobs. Today we have delayed entry into work to at least 18 by introducing the requirement to remain in learning to age 18. For almost half the school population the move into employment does not come until even later, when they are in their early 20s, as a consequence of significant increases in the proportion of pupils progressing to higher education. The initial career move for most people on leaving school today is a move not into a job but into further study, whether this is on to a course of further education or an apprenticeship at age 16 or on to a university course or higher apprenticeship at age 18. These young people will need employability skills but more urgent will be the need for the skills to succeed in further study, i.e. independent learning skills. Schools in England are very good at helping young people progress into higher education. In 2017-18 the proportion of students going on to university reached the target of 50% set by Prime Minister Tony Blair in 1999 (DfE, 2019a). However, dropout rates are too high. 1 in 16 students starting a degree course will not complete it (HESA, 2019). One of the main reasons given is that they cannot cope with independent learning. Pupils moving from schools to FE colleges at 16 or 17 experience similar difficulties as they move from an environment in which their learning has been highly structured, with weekly deadlines for submitting work, to one where they may be given several weeks to complete a project. Universities and colleges adapt their teaching approaches to help students manage their own learning but there is also a responsibility on schools to help prepare pupils for independent learning. Similar to employability skills, it is not possible to find a single list of independent learning skills but they usually include organisational, time-management, planning, target-setting, research, seeking feedback and support, self-review. These skills are equally important transition skills.

Is an overall focus on career management skills enough? As reported in Chapter 1, almost fifty years ago the Schools Council Careers Education and Guidance Project posed the question should the aims of careers education be limited to equipping pupils to make choices and manage transitions or is there a place also for helping young people understand opportunity structures and empowering them to become more proactive in forging their own careers and perhaps even influence those structures. Bill Law, to whom this book is dedicated, used to comment that a lot of careers lessons he observed were not careers *education* but were instead careers *training*. Pupils were being helped to develop the skills to secure and keep jobs within existing opportunity structures, but not being helped to understand those structures and how they might change them or create new opportunities both for their own benefit and for that of society.

Careers education should extend beyond the skills needed *for* careers and also encompass knowledge and understanding *about* careers. This involves not just providing information about opportunities in learning and work but also study of the changing nature of careers and the role that individuals' decisions about learning and work play in shaping society. Careers education in schools should both equip young people to research, plan and manage their journey through education, training and employment, and help them understand the world of work and to take control over their future pathways. In addition to gaining career management skills pupils should be empowered to overcome barriers to progression and to influence opportunity structures. More recently this debate has been revisited in the context of how careers education can contribute to social justice (Hooley, Sultana and Thomsen, 2017).

In summary, the DOTS framework of careers management skills still provides a solid foundation from which to design a careers education programme, but should be supplemented by the digital career management skills, employability skills and independent learning skills, plus an element of career studies i.e. learning about the nature of career and how opportunity structures can be influenced and changed.

The statutory position of careers education in the school curriculum

The failure to take the opportunity, presented by launching the careers strategy, to reinstate, and possibly also extend, the statutory duty to provide careers education was described in the previous chapter. Putting back in place the legal requirement to include careers education would not in itself ensure good quality provision for all pupils but it would reduce the risk of schools removing careers education from the curriculum and help ensure an entitlement to some form of careers education for all pupils. The government should still find an opportunity to give careers education statutory status and to extend the duty to provide careers education in the curriculum up to age 18, in line with both the raising of the age of participation in learning and the legal requirement to provide access to independent careers guidance. In the meantime the DfE could achieve the same end by working with Gatsby to amend the Benchmarks to include an expectation that all secondary schools should include a programme of careers education in the curriculum for each and every pupil.

The Benchmarks are not a legal requirement but the DfE expects all schools to use them to review and develop their careers programmes and under the revised inspection framework for schools Ofsted will be looking at how schools are performing against the Benchmarks (Ofsted, 2019). Most schools have now heard of the Benchmarks and are using them to drive up the quality of their careers programmes. They have the merits of being derived from international research, they are jargon-free and so easily understood and they are being championed from outside the careers sector as well as from within it. It could be argued that careers education is included in the benchmarks as Benchmark 1 requires schools to have a "stable and embedded programme of career education and guidance", but the need for a planned programme of careers education in the curriculum is more implicit than explicit. A clearer expectation is contained within Benchmark 4 but, as discussed in the previous chapter, the reference here is to cross-curricular approaches only.

The Gatsby foundation has argued that the framework of benchmarks should not be changed, in the short term at least, and there is a lot to be said for a period of stability. I am proposing an amendment, but it is an addition which does not involve removing anything that a school may already be working on. A good quality careers education programme should include both work delivered through other subjects and a discrete programme, separately timetabled, most likely within PSHE, plus several curriculum days. Benchmark 4 should, therefore, be amended by adding an expectation that "the curriculum for all pupils of secondary age should include a discrete programme of careers education" while still keeping the expectation that all teachers should link subject learning to careers.

A new framework for careers education

Since the statutory duty to provide careers education was removed in 2012 there has been no official framework for schools to use as a guide for curriculum planning. There are several different frameworks available, including the one published by the professional body for the careers sector, the CDI, but none of them have been endorsed by The Careers & Enterprise Company or the Gatsby foundation. The careers strategy does not propose a set of outcomes from a school's careers programme: the Benchmarks that form the heart of the strategy are a framework of activities that schools should put in place. Schools need as well a framework of learning outcomes in order to plan appropriate activities and to assess what pupils have gained from the programme. At present they are referring either to the CDI's framework for careers, employability and enterprise education or to the PSHE Association's programmes of study. I propose that these two professional bodies should work together to develop a new framework, building on the two existing documents and taking into account the discussion on the scope of careers education in an earlier section of this chapter.

The CDI has already incorporated employability skills but I am suggesting that the framework should also include digital career management skills, independent learning skills and career studies. It would be useful also to examine international best practice such as the various careers blueprints from the USA, Canada and Australia. A few years ago some work was done on drafting a version of Blueprint for England and it would be worth revisiting that when drafting a new framework for careers education (LSIS, 2009). If the strategy for improving career guidance overall and careers education in particular is to be fully effective all the key players will need to work together more closely and on a sustained basis. The new framework will need to be promoted by the DfE, The Careers & Enterprise Company and the Gatsby foundation, so all three stakeholders should be consulted as the framework is developed.

Previous frameworks for careers education have gone beyond listing recommended learning outcomes across the key stages, and have offered guidance on curriculum organisation. The proposed new framework should follow this approach, and provide practical advice on combining discrete and cross-curricular models, consistent with the proposed addition to Benchmark 4.

Support for careers education

One point in its history when support for careers education was at its best was during the time of the Technical and Vocational Education Initiative (TVEI), particularly during the extension phase. Every local education authority (LEA) in England was involved. All schools and colleges worked collaboratively on developments in local consortia and received funding from central government through the LEA. A national TVEI unit set the overall agenda for the development but the LEAs agreed their specific objectives with regional TVEI officers and advisers. Since then the provision of support has become fragmented and patchy, with some local authorities, LEPs and MATs more active than others.

The recent introduction of careers hubs offers the possibility of building again a national network of support for career guidance, including careers education. An interim evaluation shows that schools working in the hubs make accelerated progress against the Gatsby Benchmarks (Hutchinson, Morris, Percy, Tanner, and Williams, 2019). At the moment it is estimated that about a quarter of all schools in England are part of a hub. If the model could be funded to extend across the whole of the country we could develop a nationwide support infrastructure similar to that which existed in the TVEI era. All schools could have access to development funding through the local hub and be encouraged to work collaboratively with other schools. The hubs promote a strategic approach to the development of career guidance in schools that aligns to local priorities. It would be important to retain this dimension to their work but the local targets could be combined with specific objectives linked to national priorities. The Careers & Enterprise Company could take on a leadership role and set national targets, such as improving careers education in the curriculum for example, which the hubs would be required to address as a condition of funding. The hubs would continue to be encouraged to work with the local authorities and MATs in their area, to maximise opportunities for support to schools.

My specific proposal here is that the DfE commits funding to establish careers hubs across the country. Under the TVEI

Extension programme each LEA had a guarantee of development funding for five years. The first two phases of careers hubs have funding for two years only. My experience indicates that for any school improvement project to really take hold requires a minimum of three years. A national network of careers hubs with funding for 3-5 years would make a significant difference. However a sustained period of funding alone will not be sufficient. There will also need to be a commitment to invest in personnel to support developments at both the local and national levels. The Careers & Enterprise Company and the hubs will need to recruit staff with expertise in supporting curriculum and pedagogical developments. In the TVEI Extension programme each LEA appointed advisers and development managers for careers education and guidance and the Employment Department established a national careers education and guidance team within the TVEI central unit to drive, support and monitor developments at the local level. A similar infrastructure of support is required today.

Training for careers education

One of the strands of the careers strategy that has been particularly well received is the nationally funded programme of careers leader training. The number of schools that have registered an interest in the courses is more than twice the original number of places initially allocated. Careers leaders who are inspired and informed by good quality professional development are able to apply their training to improving the provision in their schools. The recent national survey of careers leaders provides evidence that schools whose careers leaders benefit from the training programmes achieve more benchmarks than other schools (Tanner, Percy and Andrews, 2019).

Leadership of careers includes subject leadership of careers education, so it is important that courses for careers leaders pay due attention to planning schemes of work for careers education, briefing and supporting teachers of careers lessons and monitoring teaching and learning. Case study research referred to in an earlier chapter showed the need for this training in particular for careers co-ordinators who come from professional backgrounds other than teaching (Andrews, 2005). This is even more crucial now that we know that 42% of careers leaders do not have Qualified Teacher Status (QTS). The recent national survey also showed the need for careers leaders to be given the time to fulfil their responsibilities, to be placed in an appropriate position in the management structures of the school and to be paid on a salary scale commensurate with their middle, or senior, leadership role (op.cit.).

My proposal here is simply that the national programme of careers leader training must be continued beyond its current two-year period of funding. Although a large proportion of schools will access the training in this timeframe not all schools will be able to take advantage of the courses by 2020, and there will continue to be a national turnover of staff. Indeed, it is possible that there will be an increase in the rate of turnover as careers leaders build on the successes of improving the careers programmes in their schools to develop their own careers. We have waited many years for the government to recognise the importance of appropriate training for the role of careers leader. I have said, in numerous conference speeches, that there is a deep irony in the fact that the one member of staff above all others who should be promoting the need of training and qualifications for jobs, is the one person who often has no training for their job. It would be disappointing to say the least if the programme only ran for two years. Professional development for the role of careers leader should be an embedded and sustainable feature of the permanent infrastructure, not just a short-term measure.

In addition to ensuring that the careers leader training courses continue, the next logical step would be to establish a national professional qualification for the role. The current courses are a mix of non-accredited and award-bearing programmes, provided by universities, careers training organisations and school leadership training providers. One of the universities, University of Warwick, has developed a bespoke postgraduate award for careers leadership: the others are using existing modules from their postgraduate programmes. The careers training organisations are using the CDI's Certificate in Careers Leadership which consists of three optional units from the full Level 6 Diploma in Career Guidance and Development that closely align with The Careers & Enterprise Company's specification for the training, but these were not designed as a full award. One of the school leadership training providers is exploring the possibility of accrediting its careers leader training programme through the National Professional Qualification for Middle Leadership (NPQML). It would be possible to imagine a future scenario where all three options were available – a higher education postgraduate award that could contribute to a Master's programme, a Level 6 competency-based award that could contribute to the full Diploma and the NPQML – but all developed on the same framework of learning outcomes. The learning outcomes for the qualifications could be based on the current specification for the careers leader training programme but informed also by reference to the National Occupational Standards (NOS) for Career Development for which the CDI is the guardian (CDI, 2014).

At the same time as ensuring the future of the careers leader training programme and developing a professional qualification for the role, the proposals in the Teach First report on the role of teachers in careers education should be revisited (Teach First, 2015). There is a case to be made for including an introduction to career guidance, including careers education, in all programmes of initial teacher education and then following this up with sessions on the role of the teacher in careers education in continuing professional development (CPD) for qualified teachers in their first two years of teaching. It is rare for career guidance to be given any attention in initial teacher education. It is perhaps understandable that students training to enter the profession will be more concerned about the subject content, pedagogy and assessment methods for their chosen discipline, and issues such as classroom management. Nevertheless it would be useful to at least introduce the notion that they are most likely to be asked to contribute to the school's careers programme when they take up post. Once teachers start working in schools they are provided with CPD to support the various different roles and tasks that make up their job and this would be the most appropriate point to cover in greater depth their roles as tutor and a subject teacher contributing to the careers programme. These roles should feature more explicitly in the Early Career Framework, a two-year package of structured training and support for teachers in their first years of teaching, published and funded by the DfE (DfE, 2019b). Finally it would also be helpful to include reference to the school's responsibilities for career guidance in all headteacher development programmes linked to the National Professional Qualification for Headship (NPQH).

Quality assurance

At present schools have available two means of quality assuring their careers programmes, both of which are voluntary. The Careers & Enterprise Company has worked with Gatsby to develop the Compass tool, which is an online, free of charge tool that schools can use to self-review their progress against the Benchmarks. The questions that relate to careers education are limited to ones that ask about linking subject teaching to careers plus a question about whether careers education is planned within PSHE lessons.

Schools can also choose to submit to an external assessment against the criteria for the *Quality in Careers Standard*. This involves the payment of a fee to cover the costs of the assessment visit. As described in earlier chapters, this national standard has evolved from the previous local quality awards and is now strongly recommended by the DfE. There have been discussions between the Quality in Careers Consortium and the Gatsby foundation about the relationship between the two approaches and the Quality in Careers Consortium has brought itself into line with the Compass tool by linking its assessment criteria to the Benchmarks. The *Quality in Careers Standard* has always placed a strong emphasis on schools having in place a good quality programme of careers education, and in this area the expectations exceed those of the Benchmarks. However, neither the Gatsby foundation nor The Careers & Enterprise Company currently actively promotes the *Quality in Careers Standard* as a means of externally validating a school's own assessment if it has achieved all eight benchmarks. It would be helpful if the Standard could be fully incorporated into the strategy in this way.

Of course, there is also a third dimension to quality assurance in school and that is the inspection regime administered by Ofsted. It is helpful that the revised framework for inspection that Ofsted teams have been using from September 2019 includes stronger references to career guidance, although it remains to be seen to what extent inspection teams apply this section of the framework robustly and consistently. Experience with previous versions is that, with small teams in school for only two days, career guidance does not always get scrutinised in any depth, and many schools, particularly those deemed outstanding, are visited infrequently. The stronger statements about careers will help to ensure that schools make good provision but will not guarantee it.

Development funding for schools

The new policy for careers guidance introduced in 2012 has cost schools money. Previously careers advisers from the local authorities' Connexions service came into schools to provide careers guidance to young people with no cost to the school – the service was fully funded by central and local government. From 2012 schools have been required to provide access to independent careers guidance but they have been given no additional funding to help pay for this service. Schools have had to allocate money from other parts of their budgets to either commission a careers guidance service from an external provider or employ their own qualified careers adviser.

Similarly, the careers strategy does not include any allocation of funding direct to all schools to support the development work expected by the DfE. Those schools that access places on the careers leader training programme receive a bursary of £1,000 and the training course is free of charge. The 25% of schools that are part of a careers hub may also have access to development funding through the hub, and some of the resources and activities available from The Careers & Enterprise Company are fully funded. The Gatsby pilot in the North East demonstrated that schools were able to achieve significant improvement in the provision of career guidance with relatively modest levels of development funding. Similar projects led by local authorities and LEPs have shown similar results (for example, Moore, Vigurs, Everitt and Clark, 2017). Development funding grants of a few thousand pounds could help to make a real difference in achieving the ambitions of the careers strategy.

One way of administering such financial support, and ensuring that the money would be spent on developing the careers programme, would be to make the allocation of money conditional upon a commitment from the school to work towards achieving the *Quality in Careers Standard*. The Standard encompasses fully all eight benchmarks, and includes specific requirements with respect to a planned programme of careers education in the curriculum. The DfE would have to find the money and it would probably be administered by The Careers & Enterprise Company. The funding would be available to all secondary schools in England but schools would be required to apply for it. The application would be required to include a written commitment, from the chair of governors, that the school would work towards the Standard. The money would then be paid in two instalments. A proportion of the funding, say 40%, could be transferred to the school on receipt of the application and the commitment, with the remainder payable once the school had been externally assessed as having achieved the Standard. Schools are now required to publish details of their careers programmes on their websites. These requirements could be revised to include stating whether or not the school had achieved the *Quality in Careers Standard*. This would provide a further incentive to improve the position of career guidance, including careers education.

In summary, I propose that a strategy for improving careers education in schools in England should be accommodated within an extension of the current careers strategy. The details are set out in Table 1.

Table 1. A strategy for improving careers education in schools

Action	Organisations responsible for implementation
1. Reinstate the statutory duty to provide careers education and extend the requirement to age 18	DfE
2. Amend the Gatsby Benchmarks to include an explicit expectation that schools should provide a planned programme of careers education for each and every pupil, including both work in other subjects and a discrete provision	Gatsby
3. Prepare and promote a new framework for careers education covering: self-development; career exploration; career management; career studies; digital career management skills; employability skills; independent learning skills	CDI, PSHE Association, Gatsby, The Careers & Enterprise Company, DfE
4. Extend the network of careers hubs to cover the whole country and build an infrastructure to drive developments at the local level	DfE, The Careers & Enterprise Company, LEPs
5. Continue the careers leader training programme beyond 2020 and develop a national professional qualification for careers leaders	DfE, The Careers & Enterprise Company, CDI
6. Encourage providers of initial teacher education to include an introduction to career guidance in their programmes for trainee teachers	DfE
7. Encourage all schools to include sessions on career guidance in their programmes of CPD	DfE

8. Actively promote the *Quality in Careers Standard* as an external validation of achieving all eight benchmarks (as revised)	DfE, The Careers & Enterprise Company, Gatsby, Quality in Careers Consortium
9. Make development funding available to all schools, linked to a commitment to work towards, and achieve, the *Quality in Careers Standard*	DfE, The Careers & Enterprise Company
10. Require schools to publish details of whether or not they have achieved the *Quality in Careers Standard*	DfE

Working together

Working together for a better future was the title of a short paper published by three government departments in 1987 setting out an ambition to improve programmes of careers education and guidance. The overall approach was based on partnership working, principally between schools and the careers service but also together with LEAs, colleges, universities, training providers and parents. More than 30 years later, as we implement another strategy to improve careers support for young people, some of the players remain the same while others have been replaced by new organisations but the levels of collaboration are not as strong as they need to be. The debate about career guidance in general, and careers education in particular, is characterised by too many instances of setting one organisation or individual against another, rather than bringing them together and respecting each other's contributions. If we are to bring about the improvements that are needed, including a more secure and better quality provision of careers education in schools, there needs to be more 'both…and' and less 'either…or'

Recent illustrations of differences in opinion include the following examples, all of which have been referred to in this book.

- should young people be provided with inspirational talks from employers or a careers interview with an impartial careers adviser?

- should schools have a careers leader or a careers adviser?

- at a local level should support be provided by an Enterprise Co-ordinator or a Careers Hub Lead?

- who should lead on careers education in the curriculum, the CDI or the PSHE Association?

- should careers education be delivered as discrete lessons or through a cross-curricular approach?

- should schools use the Compass tool to self-review or seek external assessment through the *Quality in Careers Standard*?

These are false dichotomies that unnecessarily consume time and energy. The answer in all cases is both. We need to muster our limited resources and work collaboratively to achieve the step change that is required. In particular this means, in the contemporary context, The Careers & Enterprise Company working closely not only with the Gatsby foundation but also the CDI and the Quality in Careers Consortium as equal strategic partners, with regular consultations with the DfE.

The place of careers education in a curriculum for the 21st century

So far this chapter has set out proposals for taking careers education forward by enhancing the current careers strategy. All the key partners need to work together to ensure that careers education has a better future so that our schools can equip future generations to make the most of their working lives. As I said at the end of the first edition there is no more important purpose to education, particularly when life expectancy continues to rise and retirement becomes delayed by increases in the age at which we become entitled to our pensions. Young people in school do not want to dwell on the end of their working lives but they do need the knowledge, understanding, skills and qualities to navigate their journey through a challenging and changing landscape of education, training and employment. This is what good careers education provides and I urge policy-makers, school leaders, careers professionals and everyone working to support career guidance in schools to act on the proposals set out here.

However, I do not want to end there. The actions I have put forward represent a pragmatic approach to securing better careers education for the present generation of young people in schools. For the longer term a more fundamental reform of the school curriculum is needed, and one which is not confined solely to improving careers support.

Throughout its history careers education has struggled to secure a firm foothold in the school curriculum. Despite headteachers and others understanding its value, careers education has all too often been pushed to the margins of the curriculum and taught by teachers who happen to have some space on their timetables. It is sometimes difficult to understand how this situation has persisted. We spend such a high proportion of our lives at work, and being employed is a major factor in determining our attachment to and participation in society, yet education about and for work represents a tiny amount of the curriculum time in schools.

The reasons for this disconnect can be found in the wider debate about the purposes of education and its relationship with employment. Watts (1985) identifies four functions which schools can play in relation to the world of work: selection; socialisation; orientation; preparation. Programmes of careers education in the curriculum contribute to all four areas by helping pupils: to understand the value of qualifications; to develop appropriate behaviours for the workplace; to understand the world of employment; to acquire employability skills. However, while the school curriculum remains dominated by a system of public examinations in which the content is heavily influenced by universities whose prime interest is preparing students for further study in those subjects, the time and space for careers education will be limited. It is possible that the introduction of T levels, the new technical and vocational qualifications which are being designed in partnership with employers, may lead to a rebalancing of the curriculum but at the moment this looks unlikely. T levels will form an alternative pathway for some students rather than a part of the curriculum for all.

The discourse can be expressed in terms of the 'cultural transmission' view of education versus the 'anticipatory value' view. The former refers to education being seen as the means by which one generation hands on to the next its cultures, i.e. its knowledge, understanding and values, while the latter refers to education being seen as equipping young people for their future lives. The debate is about intrinsic value and relevance. In response to the pupil's question "why are we doing this?", the cultural transmission answer is "because it's good for you", while the anticipatory value answer is "because it will be useful to you". The two are not mutually exclusive but from the expansion of free state education to all secondary age pupils after the Second World War, and indeed for many years before that, the cultural transmission view has been dominant. The content of the school curriculum has been based on the principles of a liberal education, in which education is valued for its own sake and personal enrichment. For many years teachers were resistant to any attempts to challenge this approach and introduce elements more directly linked to preparing pupils for the world of work.

The Great Debate initiated by Prime Minister James Callaghan's speech in 1976 was an attempt to reform the education system so that the curriculum might better prepare young people for a more technological future. As reported in the history section of this book, this was partially successful and it led to the Technical and Vocational Education Initiative (TVEI), in which greater emphasis was placed on careers education and careers guidance and counselling, alongside the introduction of more vocational courses and qualifications. Traditional school subjects still took up the majority of curriculum time, but there was a better balance between intrinsic value and relevance. Within a few years, however, the situation swung back to one in which the traditional subjects dominated the timetable. The National Curriculum, introduced in 1989, consisted of a list of subjects that would have been instantly recognisable to a teacher from a grammar school in the period before the Educational Act 1944, with the exception that design and technology and information technology had been added.

The aims of the school curriculum set out in Section 1 of the Education Reform Act 1988 that introduced the National Curriculum in England, covered both the cultural transmission and the anticipatory value views. The first aim referred to promoting the development of pupils and of society, and provided the rationale for the list of core and foundation subjects. The second aim talked about preparing pupils for the opportunities, responsibilities and experiences of adult life. Careers education was considered to be part of the second aim. Along with other areas of what is now known as PSHE education it was presented as a cross-curricular theme to be woven into the subject schemes of work. Despite several revisions to the National Curriculum, the traditional subjects still dominate the timetable, not least because it is pupils' achievements in the public examinations in these subjects that constitute the main measure of how the performance of the school is judged. When the DfE announced the review of the National Curriculum in 2011, the remit (DfE, 2011) stated that the new curriculum would have a greater focus on subject content and "should embody our cultural and scientific inheritance: the best that our past and present generations have to pass on to the next." (p.2).

We need a major reform to the school curriculum in England, in which there is not just a review of the subject content, but also an examination of the key competencies required to be an economically active and responsible citizen. The main areas of knowledge and culture should remain in place but greater emphasis should be placed on developing pupils' skills for life. There is no evidence that the current government is likely to initiate such a profound debate in the near future. As I complete this book a general election is imminent but there is such a backlog of domestic policy issues to debate, because of the inordinate amount of parliamentary time consumed by Brexit over the past three years, that it might be some time before any incoming government turns its attention to reforming the curriculum. When the time does come the careers sector needs to be ready to present its case for a more central place for careers education. Careers education needs to become a core part of the curriculum for all pupils. In the meantime we should amend immediately the current careers strategy to include the proposals put forward in this chapter, and thereby secure a stronger provision of careers education in our schools. It is what our young people both need and deserve.

References

Andrews, D. (2005). *Careers Co-ordinators and Workforce Remodelling.* Cambridge: NICEC

Career Development Institute (2014). *National Occupational Standards: Career Development.* Online: https://www.thecdi.net/National-Occupational-Standards (accessed 22 August 2019)

Department for Education (2011). *Review of the National Curriculum in England: Remit.* Online: www.education.gov.uk/schools/teachingandlearning/curriculum/nationalcurriculum/b0073043/remit-for-review-of-the-national-curriculum-in-england (accessed 2 February 2011)

Department for Education (2017). *Careers strategy: making the most of everyone's skills and talents.* Online: https://assets.publishing.service.gov.uk/government/uploads/system/uploads/attachment_data/file/664319/Careers_strategy.pdf (accessed 19 July 2019)

Department for Education (2019a). *Participation Rates in Higher Education: Academic Years 2006/2007 – 2017/2018.* Online: https://assets.publishing.service.gov.uk/government/uploads/system/uploads/attachment_data/file/834341/HEIPR_publication_2019.pdf (accessed 28 October 2019)

Department for Education (2019b). *Early Career Framework.* Online: https://assets.publishing.service.gov.uk/government/uploads/system/uploads/attachment_data/file/773705/Early-Career_Framework.pdf (accessed 28 October 2019)
Gatsby Charitable Foundation (2014). Good Career Guidance. London: Gatsby Charitable Foundation

Gatsby Charitable Foundation (2014). *Good Career Guidance.* London: Gatsby Charitable Foundation

Higher Education Statistics Agency (2019). *Non-continuation following year of entry (Table T3). UK domiciled full-time undergraduate students. Academic year of entry 2015/16 to 2016/17.* Online: https://www.hesa.ac.uk/news/07-03-2019/non-continuation-tables (accessed 28 October 2019)

Hooley, T. (2012). How the internet changed career: framing the relationship between career development and online technologies. *Journal of the National Institute for Career Education and Counselling* (NICEC). Issue 29 (October 2012)

Hooley, T., Sultana, R. and Thomsen, R. (2017). *Career Guidance for Social Justice*. London: Routledge

Learning and Skills Improvement Service (2009). *Career learning for the 21st century: the career blueprint – a competence approach*. Coventry: LSIS

Hutchinson, J., Morris, M., Percy, C., Tanner, E and Williams, H. (2019). *Careers Hubs: One Year On*. London: The Careers & Enterprise Company

Moore, N., Vigurs, K., Everitt, J., and Clark, L. (2017). *Progression for success: Evaluation of North Yorkshire's innovative careers guidance project. Final report*. Northallerton: North Yorkshire County Council

Morris, M., Simkin, C. and Stoney, S. (1995). *The Role of the Careers Service in Careers Education and Guidance in Schools*. Sheffield: Employment Department

Ofsted (2019). *The education inspection framework*. Online. https://assets.publishing.service.gov.uk/government/uploads/system/uploads/attachment_data/file/801429/Education_inspection_framework.pdf (accessed 22 August 2019)

Teach First (2015). *Careers education in the classroom. The role of teachers in making young people work ready*. London: Teach First

The Careers & Enterprise Company (2016). *Moments of Choice*. London: The Careers & Enterprise Company

The Careers & Enterprise Company (2019). *State of the Nation 2019: Careers and enterprise provision in England's secondary schools and colleges*. London: The Careers & Enterprise Company

Turner, E., Percy, C. and Andrews, D. (2019). *Careers Leaders in Secondary Schools: The first year*. London: The Careers & Enterprise Company

Watts, A.G. (1985). "Education and Employment: the Traditional Bonds". In Dale, R. (ed.) *Education, Training and Employment: Towards a New Vocationalism?* Oxford: Pergamon

Glossary of acronyms

ACEG (Association for Careers Education and Guidance) The name of the professional association for careers teachers in England and Wales from 2006 until 2013 when it merged with three other professional associations in the careers sector to establish the *Career Development Institute (CDI)*. Formerly known as the *National Association of Careers and Guidance Teachers (NACGT)*, and before that the *National Association of Careers Teachers (NACT)*.

ACPI (Association of Careers Professionals International) The membership body for careers advisers working in the private sector and with people in employment. One of the legacy bodies that merged with others to establish the *Career Development Institute (CDI)* in 2013.

AICE (Advisers and Inspectors for Careers Education) A network of advisers and inspectors with responsibility for careers education working for local (education) authorities and careers services or as independent consultants. Established in the 1980s but it has since disbanded.

AOC (Association of Colleges) The membership organisation representing further education (FE) colleges.

ATW (Active Tutorial Work) Structured programmes of *PSE* and pastoral care delivered in tutorial time and developed in the 1980s.

CAMPAG The national organisation for setting training standards in advice, advocacy, counselling, guidance, mediation and psychotherapy in the 1990s.

CBI (Confederation of British Industry) A membership organisation representing businesses in the UK.

CDI (Career Development Institute) The professional association for everyone working in careers education and guidance in the UK. Established in 2013, through the merger of four professional associations including the *ICG* and *ACEG*.

CEC (The Careers & Enterprise Company) An organisation established in 2015, and funded through a government grant plus contributions from employers and charitable foundations, to connect schools and colleges with employers and providers of careers activities to support the development of careers programmes for young people in England.

CEGNET (www.cegnet.co.uk) The website of the CEIAG Support programme.

CEIAG (Careers education, information, advice and guidance) The overarching term that was used in England prior to adopting 'career guidance'.

CELP (Careers and Employability Leaders Programme) A CPD programme for careers leaders developed by Teach First.

CPD (Continuing Professional Development) The maintenance and enhancement of the knowledge, expertise and competence of professionals throughout their careers.

CRAC (Careers Research and Advisory Centre) A charitable organisation established originally in 1964 to advise pupils, teachers and youth employment officers, it soon evolved into a research and development organisation and provider of courses and conferences.

CSNU (Connexions Service National Unit) A unit established within the *Department for Education and Skills (DfES)* to administer the Connexions service delivered by 47 local partnerships.

CYEE (Central Youth Employment Executive) The body which administered the youth employment service from 1948 until it was replaced by the careers service in the 1970s. Composed of officials from the Ministry of Labour, the Ministry of Education and the Scottish Education Department.

DBIS (Department for Business, Innovation and Skills) The government department in England that had responsibility for the adult careers services when the National Careers Service was established in 2012.

DCSF (Department for Children, Schools and Families) The name of the government department with responsibility for education in England, from 2007 to 2010.

DES (Department of Education and Science) The name of the government department with responsibility for education in England, from 1964 to 1992.

DfE (Department for Education) The name of the government department with responsibility for education in England, from 1992 to 1995 and from 2010 to the present day.

DfEE (Department for Education and Employment) The name of the government department in England with responsibility for education and employment, from 1995 to 2001.

DfES (Department for Education and Skills) The name of the government department in England with responsibility for education from 2001 to 2010, after the employment responsibilities were transferred from the former *Department for Education and Employment (DfEE)* to a new Department for Work and Pensions (DWP).

DOTS A framework for careers education comprising: decision learning; opportunity awareness: transition learning; self awareness.

EA (Enterprise Adviser) A volunteer from business who is linked to a school and gives a day a month of their time to advise the senior leadership on strategies for linking with employers to enhance their careers provision. Part of a national network co-ordinated by *LEPs* and the *CEC*.

EBPs (Education Business Partnerships) Local organisations brokering links between schools and employers.

ED (Employment Department) From the 1970s the name of the government department with responsibility for all matters related to employment. In 1995 it was merged with the *Department for Education (DfE)* to form the *Department for Education and Employment (DfEE)*.

FE (Further education) Education in addition to that provided by secondary schools but below the level of higher education. Generally available from age 16 in England although some FE colleges also offer courses for 14-16 year-old students in partnership with schools.

GCSE (General Certificate of Secondary Education) The public examinations taken by all pupils in English schools at age 16.

GEST (Grant for Education Support and Training) An annual government grant allocated to *LEAs* in the 1990s to provide and support *INSET* courses for school staff.

HMI (Her Majesty's Inspectorate, also Her Majesty's Inspector) The organisation responsible for inspecting schools in England. It also offered advice and guidance to government and to schools. Replaced by *Ofsted* in 1992.

IAG (information, advice and guidance) A term sometimes used to describe career guidance services, particularly in England for adults prior to the establishing the Next Steps service and then the National Careers Service and for young people during the Connexions era.

iCeGS (International Centre for Guidance Studies, University of Derby) An applied research centre specialising in career development and employability, established in 1998.

ICG (Institute for Careers Guidance) The professional association for careers advisers and one of the legacy bodies that merged with others to form the *Career Development Institute (CDI)* in 2013.

ICO (Institute of Careers Officers) The professional association for careers officers in the UK, which later changed its name to the *Institute for Careers Guidance (ICG)*.

ILEA (Inner London Education Authority) The *LEA* for the City of London and the 12 inner London boroughs, from 1965 to 1990.

INSET (In-service training) The term used to describe *continuing professional development (CPD)* in schools.

IT (information technology) In the context of how the term is used here, it refers to software resources used in programmes of careers education and guidance.

LEA (Local Education Authority) Locally elected bodies which have been responsible for the administration of schools from the beginning of the 20th century. More recently referred to simply as 'local authorities'.

LEPs (Local Enterprise Partnerships) Partnerships between local authorities and businesses, working together on local strategies for economic development.

MAT (Multi-academy trust) A formal partnership between groups of schools with academy status.

NACT (National Association of Careers Teachers) Established in 1964 as the professional association for careers teachers in England and Wales. In 1973 it changed its name to the *National Association of Careers & Guidance Teachers (NACGT)*.

NACGT (National Association of Careers & Guidance Teachers) The name of the professional association for careers teachers in England and Wales from 1973 to 2006, which later changed its name to the *Association for Careers Education and Guidance (ACEG)*.

NAEGA (National Association for Education Guidance for Adults) The membership body for careers advisers working in the public sector and with adult clients. One of the legacy bodies that merged with others to establish the *Career Development Institute (CDI)* in 2013.

NAO (National Audit Office) The organisation which on behalf of parliament scrutinises public spending, thereby helping it to hold the government to account and ensure value for money in public services.

NAPCE (National Association for Pastoral Care in Education) A membership organisation founded in 1982 to establish links between education professionals and allied agencies with an interest in pastoral care and *personal and social education (PSE)*.

NCC (National Curriculum Council) A non-governmental organisation established in 1988 to oversee the implementation of the National Curriculum in England. Later merged with the School Examinations and Assessment Council (SEAC), to form the *School Curriculum and Assessment Authority (SCAA)*.

NCVQ (National Council for Vocational Qualifications) A body established by government to develop a coherent national framework of vocational qualifications in England, Wales and Northern Ireland. In 1997 its functions in England were transferred to the *Qualifications and Curriculum Authority (QCA)*.

NEET (Not in Education, Employment or Training) A term used to describe mainly young people disengaged from learning and not in work.

NFER (National Foundation for Educational Research) An independent provider of research services in education.

NICEC (National Institute for Career Education and Counselling)
Originally founded as a research and development institute in
1975 it now plays the role of a learned society for researchers
and reflective practitioners in the broad field of career education,
career guidance and counselling and career development.

NOS (National Occupational Standards) Statements of the
standards individuals should achieve in order to work in the
particular sector, expressed in terms of performance criteria and
underpinning knowledge and understanding.

NPQH (National Professional Qualification for Headship) A
qualification to support the professional development of aspiring
and serving headteachers, provided by organisations accredited
by the *DfE*.

**NPQML (National Professional Qualification for Middle
Leadership)** A qualification to support the professional
development of aspiring and serving middle leaders in schools,
provided by organisations accredited by the *DfE*.

NVQ (National Vocational Qualification) Competency-based
qualifications linked to particular occupational sectors and
designed for use in work settings.

**OECD (The Organisation for Economic Co-operation and
Development)** An inter-governmental organisation of 36 member
countries established in 1961 to stimulate economic progress.
It has produced several reports on career guidance policy and
practice.

**Ofsted (Office for Standards in Education, Children's Services
and Skills)** Established in 1992, the organisation responsible for
the external inspection of all state-funded education.

PSE (Personal and Social Education) The area of the school
curriculum in England where pupils learn the knowledge, skills
and attributes they need to keep themselves healthy and safe,
and to prepare for life and work in society. Later referred to as
Personal, Social and Health Education (PSHE) and then *Personal,
Social, Health and Economic Education (PSHE Education)*.

PSHE (Personal, Social and Health Education) See *Personal and
Social Education (PSE)*.

**PSHE Education (Personal, Social, Health and Economic
Education)** See *Personal and Social Education (PSE)*.

QCA (Qualifications and Curriculum Authority) A non-governmental organisation established in 1997 from the merger of the *School Curriculum and Assessment Authority (SCAA)* and the *National Council for Vocational Qualifications (NCVQ)* to oversee all matters related to the curriculum, assessment and qualifications.

QTS (Qualified Teacher Status) The status conferred on a person who has met all the requirements to teach in schools in England .

RE (Religious education) A compulsory subject in all schools in England and Wales since the Education Act 1944

SCAA (School Curriculum and Assessment Authority) A non-governmental organisation established in 1993 from the merger of the *National Curriculum Council (NCC)* and the School Examinations and Assessment Council (SEAC), to oversee reviews of the National Curriculum and to administer the system of national assessments. Merged with the *National Council for Vocational Qualifications (NCVQ)* in 1997 to form the *Qualifications and Curriculum Authority (QCA)*.

SSAT (Specialist Schools and Academies Trust) Formerly an organisation established to support specialist schools and academies in the 2000s but since the Trust closed the acronym has been used by the Schools, Students and Teachers network which provides CPD.

SSFU (sensing, shifting, focussing, understanding) A framework for progression in career learning.

TECs (Training and Enterprise Councils) Local bodies established in England and Wales in the 1990s to administer publicly-funded training programmes. Abolished in 2001 and in England their functions were taken over the Learning and Skills Council (LSC).

TRIST (TVEI-related in-service training) Courses of CPD linked to the *TVEI* curriculum development programme.

TVEI (Technical and Vocational Education Initiative) A government programme, led by the *Employment Department (ED)*, which aimed to reform the 14-18 curriculum for all pupils to make is more relevant to working life and which ran from 1983 until the mid-1990s.

Index

careers hubs	95, 97, 112-113, 119, 133-134, 139
careers information	12-16, 25, 41-43, 46, 50, 65, 76, 127
careers leaders	84, 90, 92, 95, 104, 114-117, 119, 134-135, 139
Careers Professional Alliance	84
Careers Service	13, 21, 29, 41-45, 59, 140
careers strategy	94, 105-106, 118, 120, 124-126, 137-139, 144
careers teachers	12-20, 28-29, 37, 68, 92
Careers and Employability Leaders Programme (CELP)	93, 113
CEGNET	56, 83
Central Youth Employment Executive	13-16
Chubb, Paul	85
citizenship	54-55
classroom resources	21, 41, 65, 108
Cleaton, David	27-28
Compass	106, 111, 136-137
Confederation of British Industry (CBI)	37, 48, 110
Connexions	54, 59-61, 63, 78-80
Continuing professional development (CPD)	92-93, 108, 114, 119-120, 136, 139
CRAC	16, 20-21, 23
cross-curricular themes	34-35, 37-40, 47-48, 143
Crowley, Tony	21
Curriculum Matters series	27, 36
curriculum models	28-29, 38-40, 107-109, 119, 131-133
curriculum time	29, 50, 69, 104, 106